CHILD WITH BEHAVIOR DISORDERS

Help your ADHD Children to Manage Their Behavior, Improve Attention, Organize Time and Reduce Anxiety for Success at School and in Life.

Emily Thompson

Table of Contents

Introduction

Being the parent of a child having ADHD requires patience and understanding more than anything else. Your child is sure to need diligence and compassion. Your child is sure to push your limits on different occasions. When your child has been crying for hours on end, there may be a reason for it. When it finally happens to you, you realize how annoying it feels. Since the day he was born, your child has kept you on your toes in the sense that he is your child despite his little challenges. A child with ADHD is similar to a child with seven siblings. There is no other way you will ever be able to get anything done by yourself. Your child will demand your attention on every single matter. That is the upside of having an ADHD child.

People with ADHD have a sense of excitement, hyperactivity and a lot of energy. In a way, they are the source of happiness and hope for many people. When the switch is turned on, the whole world can change into a ball of bright colors. Parents leave the door wide open for them; they turn into the leader of the gang. They are also the best examples of free spirits. They are identified by their energy, attention difficulties, and a struggle to keep still.

If you ask parents of a child without ADHD how they feel about having a child with the condition, you will probably get a "Darn, why me!" response. Parents of ADHD children are not given credit for being parents. They are holier than thou, condescending individuals who require praise for being pregnant unless they are reasonably familiar with the condition. When one hears about ADHD, one sees a picture of an undisciplined child. The truth is far from it. These children have difficulty focusing, sitting still, and concentrating. They have problems with situations where they have to focus on one thing at a time. Their energy is an essential part of their character. It is a blessing and a curse at the same time. It is the driving force that keeps their interest in life alive.

Even though they have ADHD, they are born as leaders. Being able to control their energy is a tremendous challenge for a child with the condition. The most challenging part of having an ADHD child is managing his life. Finding ways to harness it and give him routines are essential. Although it is sometimes challenging to achieve, it is vital to do the work to maintain the relationship. Never use the ADHD comment as an excuse to turn a blind eye or be uncaring about your child. Just be your child's parent and do your best to give him the best he can have.

Behavioral management strategies can be fruitful for children of all ages, sorting from kids younger than five up to 18. Choosing behavioral management strategies that fit the situation is the first step to establishing goals. Supplements such as a decent diet and sleep schedules have a significant role in the first few moments after waking. Removing the child's access to a particular item is crucial in the management of the condition.

Rules should be set to control the situation in a relaxed manner. Suggestions based on the child's age are effective strategies for children in the age range of 21-60 months. A delay of one hour between feeding times and a half-hour earlier bedtime are the best techniques for children below 18 months of age. The methods to use are a must to achieve these goals.

Since the child may get frustrated quickly, please do not do anything to add to his frustration. If he or she is frustrated, the process of handling the situation will not succeed.

If the ADHD child is usually active, it is best to develop an exercise schedule for him. Exercise is very beneficial. Exercise also helps him to improve his attention and concentration.

It is crucial to give the child with ADHD a lot of love and security. All parents will go through different inconsistent parenting styles. However, it is essential always to be the parent and continue to parent your child. It is also necessary to be sensitive and loving to your child.

These strategies are beneficial for parents of ADHD children. ADHD is not a disability that cannot be managed. ADHD children need to receive proper treatment. Treatment is available to help children who have ADHD. Most ADHD children whose parents receive adequate therapy will be able to control their condition. Treatment allows them to develop self-help skills to improve how they deal with their daily lives. Treatment does not cure the situation, but it helps the children to control it. As an adult, the disorder can be controlled with the right kind of treatment.

Honest and fair medication for ADHD children can be significant. Although ADHD is not a disability, counselling is also essential. The basics of counselling are honesty, compassion and consistency. Since it is not a disability, one can receive counselling from others or professionals. It is also not difficult to find a person with the same condition as yours or a professional who manages the situation. It is just essential to find the right treatment. Treatment helps to improve the ADHD child's performance in many ways. However, when treating a child, proper counselling methods must be selected. Treating dosage is often a difficult task. Opioids can be very dangerous and addictive. Benzos can cause problems with memory and concentration. One should seek a course of counselling before going ahead with any medication.

In children, these symptoms can cause problems in their adulthood. It is essential to seek a course of treatment before it becomes too late. ADHD symptoms usually appear within the first three years of a child's life. As one grows up, the symptoms of the condition will consume him or her. It is a better idea to seek a cure as soon as it dawns on a child's mind. When a parent gets a diagnosis, they should seek courses of treatment as quickly as possible.

Many children with ADHD find it difficult to stay on a schedule.

The disorder can cause many problems with a child's daily schedule. To help your child, it is essential to create a plan to make your child more responsible for his chores. Being consistent with your child's schedule also improves his performance at school.

Children with ADHD require one to create positive family routines. Children with ADHD must be allowed to do what they want to do in life. The child should be allowed to follow his or her inclinations without any struggle.

Being a parent to a child with this kind of disorder is not easy because they frequently need rules and guidance. To help manage your child's ADHD, it is essential to create a favorable schedule for him.

Because children with ADHD are naturally more fidgety than normal children, parents must create a schedule that meets their child's concentration level.

You may find yourself overwhelmed by a child with ADHD, and you cannot keep up with his or her schedule or are unorganized. Use a planner or calendar to keep everything in order.

Creating a Schedule for a Child with ADHD is a struggle for many parents. Children with ADHD have lots of energy and can be fidgety. You must provide a schedule that the child can follow when being productive.

PART I: Psychotherapy for ADHD – What Works and What Doesn't for ADHD

Chapter 1: Parent Training – Psychological and Behavioral Interventions

Parental Tips and Tools

Being the parent of an ADHD child needs thoroughness and understanding more than anything else. Your child is sure to push you to your limits on different occasions. The various ADHD behaviors can be frustrating for you. Several alternative ways that you can make life at home better for your child and the family. Behavior management goes beyond the therapy sessions with your ADHD child. Managing the behaviors at home can be challenging, but it is doable. These tips and tools will help you manage and cope with ADHD at home.

• Acceptance – You have to accept that your child has ADHD. It means that he is not exactly like other children or even his siblings. Acceptance is essential to your child because he needs to know that he is loved, no matter what. That is challenging for a parent to believe that their child has a disorder. However, the quicker you accept the diagnosis, the faster you can start modifying behaviors with your child.

• Rules – At home, you have to define the rules clearly. With an ADHD child, you cannot merely say that running is not allowed. Your child needs clear, precise rules for the home. The right thing to do is to write them down and display the rules in a prominent place in the house. Your child will have a visual imagination to remind him of the rules at all times.

• Be consistent – As mentioned earlier, consistency is the key to modifying behaviors. You must follow through on both rewards and consequences. ADHD children need consistency in their lives. They need to know that when a parent says something, it will happen. Failing to follow through is only going to make your ADHD child not trust your word. He is more likely to push those boundaries to see how far he can go.

• Routines – ADHD children thrive with routine schedules. You must establish a way for your child that you can both adhere to every day. The daily routines do not necessarily have to be the same. For instance, weekday routines and weekend routines can differ. The important thing is that you follow these routines every day and every week. Practices become habits, and you want your ADHD child to establish good habits. Prepare a written schedule your child can look at whenever he needs a reminder about what he should be doing.

• Immediate rewards and consequences – When managing ADHD at home, you have to give a quick response to your child's behaviors. You cannot wait to provide him with a consequence because he may not even remember what happened. The same is true for rewards. He needs to know right away when he does something positive or something negative. The immediate reactions will begin to mold his behaviors at home.

• Be positive – As a parent, you need to look at every situation with a positive attitude. Deal in a supportive manner in terrible cases. Your ADHD child needs encouragement for even the little things. Positivity will help your child have better self-esteem and build confidence. Just make sure that you are not putting too much pressure on your child by being positive about everything. You can support him when he has a behavioral mishap without making him feel like it is okay to behave negatively.

• Be flexible – Yes, your child needs rules and structure, and routine. He will thrive with a schedule. However, this is an ADHD child you live with, and you must allow room for flexibility. Every rule or routine has no guarantee that it will always be followed without problems. Prepare for the unexpected so that when it happens, you are ready. There will be many times when your child will need gentle reminders before you start handing out consequences. Remember: you are not perfect, and you should not expect perfection from your ADHD child.

• Stay Organized – Lack of organization will only slow down your child's progress. He is easily distracted and forgetful. Therefore, he needs his living space organized in a way that enhances his life. One thing you can do is manage his bedroom. Use baskets with labels to make sure he knows where all of his things belong. Create a quiet place for homework that is free from distractions. Think of it like this: your ADHD child's mind is already in an almost constant state of disarray and disorder. A peaceful, organized environment at home can help calm his mind.

• Cut down on screen time – Children enjoy gaming and television. While there is no need to cut off-screen time altogether, you do need to control it. Encourage activities outside—Play board games with the family. Keep your child active and engaged to prevent boredom. Do not let the PS4 or cable television become a babysitter for your child. Sure, it might give you a few moments of peace, but is it helping your ADHD child? Consider using screen time as a part of positive reinforcement. For example, your child can earn extra time on his favorite video game by achieving weekly goals.

• Interaction – Another vital tool for living with an ADHD child is to interact with him. Talk to your child. Listen to his thoughts and ideas. Ask him about his day at school if your child seems distracted hold his hands and look into his eyes. This way, he knows you are listening. Play games together. Have him help you with the dishes, house cleaning. Something that involves attention and movement. Spend some quality time with your child. No child, with ADHD or not, likes to feel ignored by their loved ones. Make time every day to interact one-on-one with your child.

• Sleep routines – So many ADHD children have trouble sleeping. Since sleep is the body's way of healing and recharging for the following day, it is obvious why it is so important. Create a nightly routine that will help your child relax, fall asleep, and stay asleep. Sleep sounds playing in the background can be helpful. A calming lavender bath before bedtime is relaxing. Follow the routine each night to help your child establish a sleep pattern that lets him get the rest that he needs.

• Learn how to say yes – It is easy for all parents to fall into the habit of always saying no to a child's request. Make an effort to start saying yes to reasonable offers. If your ADHD child still hears you telling him no, he is more likely to rebel against you. Listen to your child's requests and pay attention. For instance, is a late-night snack going to cause some sort of problem for your child? Even when you have to say no, talk about your decision with your child. Explain why you are saying no instead of just expecting him to accept it.

• Be prepared – Do not expect your child to behave all of the time. It merely is not going to happen, especially with an ADHD child. It is right in and out of the house. Before you and your child go to the store or visit a friend, sit him down and make a plan. Discuss your expectations for his behavior during the outing and discuss the consequences and rewards. Your ADHD child always needs to know what he can expect. Learn to see the signs of when your child is about to have a meltdown. It is still easier to stop it before it gets started.

Taking Care of the Parent

All of this time, we have focused on what you can do for your ADHD child. But you are only human. You have to incorporate self-care into your life, too. Living with an ADHD child is not easy. You are going to be pushed to your limits, feel overwhelmed and frustrated. You are likely to lose your temper. Just as you need to know when your child is about to lose control, you must recognize those signs within yourself. The following tips will help you take the best care of yourself to take the best care of your child.

• Take a break when you feel yourself reaching your limits. It is essentially giving yourself a time-out. Parents get stressed and overwhelmed, too, especially when dealing with ADHD. Do not let ADHD control every aspect of your life. Instead, walk away from a challenging situation and give yourself time to calm down. When you are calm, you can return to the condition with a clear head and better determine how to handle it.

• To get calm, try meditation or even the "count to ten" method. Deep breathing and also other relaxation techniques will help you get back in control of your own emotions. Remember that your ADHD child is watching you. He needs to see that even you, the parent, get frustrated. He needs to know how you deal with the emotions, and he can even learn how to calm himself with you. Come up with a code word that puts the situation or argument on hold while the two of you get centered and refocused. If he is on the verge of an outburst, and you can feel your nerves reaching their limit, use the code word to signal to hit the pause button while both of you use relaxation and calming techniques to regain control of emotions. Then, both of you will come back to the scenario with a calm, clear mind.

• Ask for help when you need it. You need time for yourself. Do not be afraid to make that time for yourself by enlisting in the service of your family or even a babysitter. As long as everyone understands your ADHD child's needs, there is nothing wrong with letting someone else take over for a little while. Give you the chance to get out and recharge. Go to the gym or take a walk. Go and watch movies or treat yourself to a manicure and pedicure.

• Utilize therapy options for yourself. Talking over ADHD issues with a professional can be quite helpful in reducing stress. A professional can give you proven advice and techniques to use at home. Even venting to a friend can help. While your friend may not have useful advice for you, getting things off your chest can be an excellent stress reliever. You do not need to keep your thoughts and feelings bottled up inside. Find a safe environment to let them out.

•   A happy, healthy parent is vital to treating ADHD and living with the accompanying behaviors. Take care of yourself, especially when you need it. Make time every week just for you. Go ahead and take that long bubble bath. The better you are, the better your child is likely to be.

Chapter 2: Behavior Management Strategies for Children with ADD/ADHD

M any medical professionals agree that developing consistent and effective behavior management techniques is essential for managing an ADD/ADHD disorder when raising children. Applying behavioral strategies is necessary for parenting in the home, modifying or managing behavior in the classroom, or particular education placement. Behavioral management strategies can be useful for infants of all ages, sorting from kids younger than five up to 18. The modelling principles here are the same as with any child: immediately reinforce positive behavior with reward or praise and curb bad behavior by allowing consequences to develop naturally.

When it comes to children that are five or younger that may be displaying beginning symptoms of ADD/ADHD, it's imperative to provide a structured and routine environment throughout the week. Be sure to let the child know beforehand if something in the usual routine is going to change. It helps young children to have expectations, boundaries, and develop trust at this age. Making a habit of giving these children instructions and preparing them beforehand makes simple and complex tasks easier to accomplish.

As your child grows to ages 6-9 years, creating a precise and predictable reward or merit system is an effective way to model positive behavior. Make it centered on time doing a favorite activity as opposed to providing candy or snacks. Provide the child with a steady diet of learning activities like reading and puzzles instead. Be sure to participate in the young child's activities since they are learning the most from you. Several parents find it helpful to use a timer to provide more structure to the child's schedule. Setting time limits beforehand will help the child expect time limits on both fun and tedious activities. This method is beneficial when the child receives a reward at the end of the predetermined time limit. It also gives them a deadline or ending for how long they have to focus on one thing before going on to another.

Older children up to age 12 still need clear instructions daily. A predetermined reward system also works well for this age group. It's essential to have a predetermined or private approach to disciplining negative behavior to avoid the embarrassment that a sensitive child with ADD/ADHD may experience. Keep an open communication line with the child's teachers to identify and address behavior problems before any classroom situations get out of control. This preemptive approach will also help mitigate the teachers' likelihood of getting frustrated with the child's ADD/ADHD disorder.

In addition to looking at how ADD/ADHD can be managed at different ages, there are common behavioral issues that many parents struggle with. Here are some ideas and strategies to try implementing at home with your child.

Managing Impulsivity

Children with ADD/ADHD are very impulsive and do not always think before they act. While it may seem like they are purposely defying you, they have difficulty controlling their impulses in reality. To help teach your child to think before they act, if they are about to do something they know is wrong, tell them to stop and think. Teach them to count to themselves, to five or ten, depending on their age, while taking deep breaths. It brings oxygen into the brain and will help them think clearly. Then have them ask themselves, what will happen if I do this? Repeat this process with your child. You teach them to control their impulsivity, regain control of their body and mind through deep breathing, and help them understand the consequences of their actions.

High Energy Levels

Children with ADD/ADHD typically have higher energy levels than those of other children. It can sometimes get them into trouble, especially if they are bored. When they are bored, they will find something to do, whether it's appropriate or not. The key to curbing behavior is to keep your child busy and active. Sign them up for sports, take them on outings to the park, or play catch with them in the backyard. Children with ADD/ADHD need this positive outlet for all of their energy. Try to find other fun activities in your community that you can participate in. Many places offer fun activities for children and families if you can do a little research. By continually keeping your child busy with festive activities, you will reduce the boredom and tendency to find activities on their own.

Forgetfulness

While all children need reminders to bring their lunch to school or comb their hair, children with ADD/ADHD will need more. They may have the good intention of going upstairs to get their jacket, only to be distracted by the toys in their room. Understand that they are not trying to aggravate you but will simply need gentle reminders. If you've sent your child up for their jacket, and they are taking too long, you can say, "Jacket," up the stairs to help them get back on track. Visuals may also work well with assisting them to remember. If they always have to bring certain things to school, you could create a visual that they place by their backpack. Every day before they leave, they have to check that visual. Now, you may have to remind them to prevent it, but then part of the responsibility goes back to them.

Focus and Concentration

While each child with ADD/ADHD will struggle with this, you can provide an environment that can help them as a parent. Take the time, observe when your child is most alert during the day and which times they may struggle. Perhaps some specific triggers or transitions cause your child to be very distracted. For example, it could be when they first arrive home from school, or when you go somewhere out of the ordinary that's not in the routine. Once you are aware of these times or triggers, work around them, so your child is doing their schoolwork at times when they are at their best. It is also a good idea to create a free working environment from other distractions, such as toys, TV, or video games. Working together with your child on homework or schoolwork will also help keep them on track. Allowing your child to be active and move around the room will also aid in concentration or learning. If your child is a wiggler, try having them sit on an exercise ball while doing their work. They can continuously be rocking and moving while working.

These are just a few ideas to try when working with a child who has ADD/ADHD. Try to individualize these approaches, depending on your child's needs and what seems to be working for your family. Don't hesitate to ask for professional assistance if you need help improving the child's behavioral management strategies with ADHD. Many specialists will come into the home and work with the family on behavior management strategies. Over time, as you implement these strategies, you can begin to see positive changes in your child's behavior.

Chapter 3: Multi-Modal Treatment

W e know three core forms of treatment can assist ADHD patients: medication, behavior modification and a mixture of both. Multi-modal treatment for an ADHD patient means employing a mix of different strategies and techniques to manage the disease's symptoms.

Applying a variety of treatments to children offers a better chance of overcoming the condition. Many forms of behavioral therapy do not require the use of medication, and I will discuss each one in detail, so you have an understanding of the service and effects of each. You can suggest these behavior modification treatments to your doctor, who will be able to explain further which treatments are most suitable for your child. All these treatments have been used and studied by many psychiatrists in the past.

Behavioral Modification

Therapists have been employing Behavior Modification treatments in the management of ADHD for the past three decades. These techniques have gained much respect over this period due to their experience and their curing for many children of aggressive and disruptive behavior. Children with ADHD have learned to manage their actions and develop positive social skills and academic performance with these methods' help. Behavior Modification treatments for children with ADHD could be divided into five categories:

- Cognitive Behavioral Interventions
- Clinical Behavior Therapy

- Direct Contingency Management

- Intensive Behavioral Treatments

- Combination of Behavioral and Pharmacological Treatments

Cognitive Behavior Therapy

Often abbreviated to CBT, this kind of treatment is perfect for parents wishing to be closely involved and active in their child's clinical development. CBT's focus is to train parents and other caregivers in the management of children's ADHD symptoms. CBT usually entails training programs, or individual sessions, in which a therapist will discuss how you can modify your child's behavior.

One of the characteristics of being the parent of an ADHD child is that it raises many doubts, irrational thoughts and expectations. While other therapies focus on direct actions, CBT helps you eliminate the roadblocks that prevent you from helping your child overcome his symptoms of ADHD. Many parents I talk to, concerning ADHD and their child, admitted to the following habits when assessing their child's development:

- Over-generalization – these parents believe that a single negative aspect of ADHD is more significant than anything else. Thus, they can overlook substantial broader progress that's taking place.

- All or nothing – if it doesn't work correctly, then it doesn't work at all! Parents need to recognize that each milestone reached is perfect in its way. There's no such thing as "all or nothing" when treating ADHD. It pays to be patient.

- "Should" thinking – this kind of thought process leads to self-resentment when you fail to do something you think you should do? But there are no "shoulds." Just keep doing what was asked or advised by the professional, and don't create further stress yourself by constantly researching what else you might do to help your child.

- Comparative thinking – this can be a poison for the mind. When you find you are comparing yourself negatively with other parents with an ADHD child, you need to remember that every ADHD case is different.

- Personalization – you take your child's disease personally. You can ask questions like, "What did I do to deserve this?" or decide, "This is karma doing its work." It's not your fault, your life is difficult, or that your child has ADHD (unless you did not take care of yourself during pregnancy). So don't take things personally.

With CBT's help, once you realize such thoughts as disabling, you can confidently eliminate them and focus on the real agenda. You must understand that to make an effective change in your child's life and mind; you need to change your thoughts.

Cognitive Behavioral Interventions

This method is commonly known as CBI. CBI's goal is to focus on self-control by using verbal self-instruction and strategies for problem-solving, self-monitoring and evaluation, cognitive modelling, and similar techniques. Your child will be scheduled a meeting with a therapist, once or twice a week, to teach these strategies through methods like role play.

One popular CBI technique used by therapists teaches a child to tell himself to "stop" when he is disruptive. Introducing these self-instruction techniques is that children with ADHD lack the motivation to give themselves cues on what or what not to do. Cognitive Behavioral Interventions are less popular today because ADHD experts have focused on developing alternative techniques.

Contingency Management

Known as CM, this type of behavioral treatment involves

a structured format that may include a special classroom for treatments. One of the main principles used in CM is the encouragement of actions through positive or negative reinforcement. It involves using economic tokens, or the giving or withholding of rewards, as behavioral tools. Though most parents are accustomed to using reward systems with their child, it can help to know the most effective ways of achieving results. Once your child has received CM treatment, he will be more able to respond correctly to your cues and the prohibitions and privileges you give him.

Intensive Behavioral Treatments

It involves the collaboration of children, parents, and teachers to apply techniques that reward children for good behavior. The combination of methods is geared towards improving socialization, self-control, and academic skills. By the end of Intensive Behavioral Treatment, your child will be able to attend school and perform better willingly.

Several Intensive Behavioral Treatment Summer Camps are available, lasting for about eight weeks, perfectly timed before the school term starts. The typical mix of behavioral treatment and recreational activities at these camps ensures kids benefit and enjoy the therapy.

Combination of Pharmacological and Behavioral Interventions

The combination of both medicinal and behavioral treatment has been useful for many ADHD children in the past. It is more effective than either behavioral or medication treatment alone. If both medication and behavioral therapy are being used, therapists typically will decrease the times, doses, and medicines during behavioral sessions. However, note that decisions on the best use and combination of treatments will always depend on the individual patient.

Effects of Medication on Children with ADHD

Significant side effects of ADHD medication you should consider is its impact on motor activity and coordination. With medication treatment, you may notice your child has a reduced activity level in school. It means he does not run around as much as he did before. Moreover, you will also notice improvements in the neatness of your child's handwriting. Similar improvements will appear in other arts and crafts activities too. Your child can play with clay, building blocks, and other constructive toys much better.

When it comes to cognitive effects, you will notice your child has a better attention span. He will no longer be so easily distracted. He will be able to focus on instructions better. He will also show a decrease in impulsivity and an increase in his productivity. When asked to do something, he is likely to do it with care and finish the task well. You will notice that accuracy and speed in working improve remarkably. When you have the moment to reflect on the degree to which medication allows new information to sink into your child's brain, you can see how beneficial meditation can be.

And the essential effect of all medication is its impact on social behavior. Being able to interact better with other individuals is vital in dealing with ADHD. Under ADHD medication, children no longer seek attention in the classroom from other children and educators because they stop their inattentive, off-task behaviors. And when mixing with other people, they exhibit less anger and more self-control. Their social skills can improve so dramatically you may include your child in organized sports, like basketball or soccer, without concern. Aggression and oppositional behavior are reduced, bossiness disappears, and such children now start to consider others' opinions.

Chapter 4: Parenting Strategies for Kids with ADHD

W hen a child gets diagnosed with ADHD, parenting goes to a whole new level. Regular tasks can turn into struggles. Your life can become chaotic if you let your feelings, especially your frustrations; show a negative impact on your daily routine. Most parents are undoubtedly right. But to be a parent to a child or teenager who has ADHD, you have to be more than just good.

Don't despair!

It's not an easy job, it's hard, but you can make things a little easier for you and your child with the following tips and strategies.

Acceptance Is Key to a Better Life with Your Child

It's a given that your child gets loved by everyone in the family. But accepting him and his situation is an entirely different thing. Parents and other family members should make him feel taken as resentment towards his disorder (not necessarily your child) puts him at risk for low self-esteem.

Don't negatively think of his inexhaustible energy. One parent whose child has ADHD says she's even jealous of his enthusiasm and can think of unusual careers he can have in the future.

Stay Calm and Focused

Dealing with children whose anger escalates quickly can indeed be very frustrating. But just like everyday parenting, showing an agitated child that you're spiralling out of control has a negative impact. Instead of "intimidating him to stop what he's doing," the results can backfire. Watch yourself closely, especially if your initial reaction is to react negatively.

Take note that trying to reason out with your child will only have adverse effects. While doing his homework, for example, he'll be making a lot of fuss. By arguing with your child and telling him to "stop complaining," you'll only be setting yourself up for a trap. Preparation time will extend, and when you're pressed for time to do other chores, anger can escalate rather quickly.

To diffuse the situation, acknowledge his frustration and give him a gentle touch. Avoid yelling at him or even chastising him for "dawdling."

Control Yourself and Be a Good Role Model

As parents, you are naturally your child's influential role models. Children will follow anything you say or do. Keep yourself in check, especially if you're angry. Yelling at your child makes him think that it's okay to do the same thing as well. The need to exercise self-control is crucial, especially in this situation. You can't expect your child to be calm when he sees you out of control as well.

Most parents think that being loud can intimidate their children. Take a step back and examine the situation, just as you would do when you get into conflicts with your co-workers or friends. Understandably, you can't avoid being angry at your child, but you can certainly stop shouting at him continually.

The second time you're angry, take a few deep breaths or leave the room. If you have techniques that help soothe you when you're mad at work, use them. Showing the importance of self-control makes it easier to help them manage their emotions as well.

Help Your Child, But Set Limits

We always want to rescue our children whenever they're in a rush. It can harm their independence. The more you do things for your children, the more they will rely on you and the less they'll do for themselves.

Be supportive, but let your child do specific tasks by himself. For instance, when it comes to homework, encourage him to work on it without your help. If you have to monitor him, then don't hover. Sit near him, and work on your own. It is an excellent time to tackle unfinished reports, update your blog, and the like.

Don't Underestimate Your Child

You get hurt when the staff at school labels him as a slow learner. Sometimes, out of frustration, you might just believe it. You shouldn't. After all, a child with ADHD is not necessarily a slow learner. His mind just doesn't work like the other children's. He can still be successful if you give him a little challenge. Those negative remarks might push you to pull him out of school and teach him yourself. But it would help if you stopped yourself from doing that.

One thing you can do is find an appropriate school for him. A public school might not be the best solution, and maybe, a school for children with special needs won't do him any good either. Instead, aim for schools that have higher expectations, a place where he gets challenged positively.

Additionally, introduce your child to the power of making sound choices. Besides preparing him to be self-reliant, he exercises control when he gets a chance to make a wise decision. There is a technique that works well in such circumstances, and that is well known as "structured choice."

For Example:

You may ask:

"Do you want to work on math questions or your science assignment first?"

"We need to put your toys back before we go out. Do you want to pick them up from the floor first, or start with the ones on your bed?"

Know the Difference Between Discipline and Punishment

Most parents would not know the difference. To discipline a child, explain what would happen if they break a rule and the rewards they can get if they continue to be on their best behavior. Explaining to them about inappropriate behavior is discipline.

Avoid yelling, threatening, taking away toys, and spanking if you haven't presented anything to him.

That's not discipline!

That's verbal and physical abuse and will not work at all. The punishment that uses fear to make your child listen to you does not work.

Focus on Teamwork with Your Child

Just as you would work things out with your spouse or co-workers to agree, you should be doing the same thing with your child. It's natural to expect him to break some rules, the same thing that other children will do. Remember, you're not perfect, and neither is your child.

When it comes to facing negative behavior consequences, work with your child to avoid such a situation.

You might say:

"What will Mommy do if you won't put your toys back after playing with them?" He will respond with a "punishment" he deems appropriate for his bad behavior (i.e., five minutes' time-out). In that way, he won't feel that you're punishing him. He'll be able to recognize what he did wrong and submit himself to the consequences.

You should also set up "mini rewards" for his excellent behavior. For example, in this simple way if he picks up his toys after playing with them without being told to do so, reward him with an extra hour of playing video games.

Separate the Disorder from the Child

You should remember that he's not precisely defiant just because "he wants to." Take note that with ADHD, being distracted or inattentive is one of the symptoms. When you tell your child to fix his bed and find him in front of the computer with the bed unmade, remind him about your request.

It's incredibly frustrating if you have to repeat what you said several times, but you shouldn't resort to calling him lazy, a slob, space, or other negative words you can think of. Avoid screaming about having to pick up his toys because he won't listen and even stop yelling about his assignment mistakes.

Instead, use the teamwork technique to solve a problem. "We have a problem with your toys, and I need your help to solve it."

Research More About ADHD

Parents need to understand their children's behavior to help them fight the battle. That's why there is a variety of support groups for parents who have children with ADHD. Aside from that, there's an influx of reliable sources on the Internet to help you figure out your child.

Knowledge is power!

When you know more, you'll find out that you're able to handle the situation better. You can anticipate problems that might lead to potentially harmful behavior.

Anticipate and Avoid Problems

Go over the rules before you go inside a grocery store or anywhere public. Make sure to talk to them about plans as well.

For example:

If you're at a party and you're starting to realize that there's a potential problem that's about to explode, ask to speak to him calmly.

You may take him from the group or leave earlier (depending on what you agreed on).

Take Care of Yourself

Ask help from family members and close friends when you need some time off. You must have alone time to help you manage the stress.

Find ways to help reduce stress:

- Reading books
- Watching a movie
- Having a cup of coffee in a quiet place

Your health is important; getting enough rest, eating the right food, and exercising keeps you healthy and strong.

Best of all, cut yourself some slack and understand that you are not a magician, nobody's perfect, and know the value of a reliable support system.

Chapter 5: Tools for Teaching Social Skills

Improving the Social Skills of Children with ADHD

Some skills are quantifiable during a child's development phase—language skills, math skills, etc. But what about the softer skills which, like social skills, do not come as naturally? ADHD kids also find it challenging to make friends and establish relationships. Some parents wonder how social skills can be developed but often don't know where to start.

Children with ADHD are no different than children without— all of them want to be liked, want to be part of a group, and want to make friends—they just do not know how. But all is not lost— there are strategies that you can do to help your child develop and being happy with his social skills as will benefit him or her as he grows up.

Increasing a Child's Social Awareness

According to various researches on ADHD, children with this disorder can be low monitors of their social behavior. They often do not have clarity on the awareness or understanding of social situations and the reactions they provoke from people around them. To them, a peer interaction went well, but, or to the other person; it did not.

An ADHD child's interaction with a peer may have gone well, but it did not. It is another example of an ADHD-related issue. According to the social setting, the ADHD child cannot accurately 'read' social situations, self-monitor themselves, and adjust their actions and behaviors. These skills would need to be taught directly to them.

Teach Skills Directly and Practice, Practice, Practice

Learning from past experiences also makes it a little more challenging when it comes to children with ADHD. They often react without thinking, but one way to remedy this would be to continually provide feedback immediately whenever a child's behavior is inappropriate or has had social miscues. Role-play is a beneficial and helpful way of shaping, teaching, and practicing positive social skills and providing the child with ways to deal with difficult situations, such as bullying and teasing.

As a parent, you can start by focusing on one or two main areas that your child struggles with the most regarding social interactions. It creates a learning process that is not too overwhelming both for child learning and parent teaching.

Often, children with ADHD have problems with the fundamentals of social exchanges such as:

- Starting and maintaining a conversation

- Interacting with people in a proper way

- Personal distance when talking

- Giving and receiving input

- Listening and asking for ideas

- Taking turns talking in a conversation

- Showing interest

- Negotiating and resolving a conflict

- Speaking using a normal tone

Identify your child's social rules and behaviors clearly and give them information. Practice these prosocial abilities repeatedly.

With immediate rewards, this will form positive behaviors.

Improving Your Child's Social Skills at Home

Learning social skills and knowing how to navigate different social rules can be challenging for kids with ADHD. Follow these tips on helping him develop better listening skills, learning to read facial expressions and gestures, and having better interactions in social situations:

• In a gentle but honest manner, let your child know about his challenges and the changes he can make.

• In selecting playmates for your kid, be careful to choose those with physical and language skills similar to his.

• In the beginning, keep invitations for having your kid's friends over down to one or two. Pay close attention to them while they are playing. Don't tolerate any yelling, pushing, and hitting.

• Have role-playing sessions with your kid, in which you act out different social scenarios. Make sure to trade roles frequently and to have fun in the process.

• Make it a priority to let your child play and reward him often to show good behavior while at play.

School Intervention Approach

The school intervention approach in behavioral therapy treatment of ADHD in kids involves helping teachers meet their educational needs by managing ADHD behaviors inside the classroom.

Your child's condition gets in his way of learning—he can hardly absorb a lesson. He can leave his work unfinished because he is either busy tuning out what he should be listening to or is too preoccupied with jumping around the classroom. And all of these should not be a surprise, like the things your child has to do in school—listening quietly, sitting still, concentrating, and following instructions—are the same things that they find quite challenging to do. This is really not because they do not want to do these things, but because they cannot do these things.

But your child with ADHD has all the right to achieve success in school, with the combined help of his parents and teachers. Here are different strategies you can try:

Ask your child's teacher to:

• Find ways to lessen potential distractions in the classroom. It would be preferable to always seat kids with ADHD, especially those who have difficulty focusing, near the teacher. The teacher may also stand near the student while giving out directions; this way, there are fewer barriers and distractions for the student to overcome in absorbing what is being said.

• Make room for movement. Let your child fidget in his seat or move around the classroom by setting up reasons for them to move. It would be great to give kids with ADHD the opportunity to get drinking water, do an errand for the teacher, make a trip to the bathroom, or any other task that requires physical action. The teacher may also let a child with ADHD keep a squeeze ball or another small object in his desk, which he can quietly manipulate without distracting his classmates.

• Make way for transitions. Ask the teacher to remind your child about an upcoming task or activity, be it recess, next class, or time for another book. It would be great if the teacher also gives lots of reminders and advance notice for field trips and other special school events. Before the day ends, the teacher may also help your kid prepare to go home by reminding him about the items he needs to accomplish his homework.

• Allow for some playtime. It helps your child enjoy his free time during recess instead of using it to work on a missed assignment. Playing during break helps him improve his focusing ability.

Be Your Child's Teacher's Partner

• Engage in regular communication with your child's teacher about his difficulties.

• Assist your child as he organizes his papers before doing homework before heading for school the next morning.

• Check if he has finished his homework in subjects with difficulties, especially if he is on the brink of failing in class.

• If necessary, request for the teacher to use a daily/weekly report.

• Make sure your kid's ADHD medication is doing what it is supposed to do when your kid is in school, and while he does his homework.

• See to it that your child places his finished homework in the right folder/organizer.

• Until the school semester ends, make sure to save all of your child's completed homework.

Turn Learning into a Fun Activity

• Use physical motion when introducing a lesson in class.

• Make up silly songs to make the details of a new lesson easier to keep in mind.

• Make dry facts more exciting and more likely to be remembered by connecting them to trivia.

Make Math Enjoyable

• Play games that make numbers so much fun for your child. You can play dominos, dice, and memory cards to make math enjoyable for your kid, or you might just wiggle or tuck in your fingers as you help your kid add and subtract.

• Make up silly acronyms. These will help your child

remember the math rules on operations, divisibility, etc.

• Draw illustrations that can help your child understand different mathematical concepts, such as word problems.

Make Reading Irresistible

• Read to your child and make sure to make reading time cozy for both of you.

• Act out what you just read together. Allow your child to pick his preferred character in the story to act out. Ask him to choose your personality, as well. Bring the story to life by using costumes and amusing voices.

• Make bets with your child. Ask him always about how he thinks the story will unfold. For example, say "The boy in the book sure seems courageous; I bet he will be the one to save the whole town!"

Getting Things Organized

• Set up a folder to hold all of your child's completed homework. It would be a great idea to organize open files in color-coded folders and to demonstrate to your child the proper way of filing.

• Have extra sets of school materials and textbooks at home, if possible.

• Assist your child in organizing his belongings in his backpack, pockets, and folders every day.

• Teach your child how to make checklists, then help him learn how to use them. Remind him to cross off an item as soon as he accomplishes it.

Getting Homework Done

• Establish a specific time and place for your child to do his homework. Get rid of the TV, pets, and other possible distractions.

• Use timers and an analogue clock in teaching your child about the course of time. These devices will also help you monitor how efficient your child is in doing his homework.

• Let your child take a break from doing homework every 10 to 20 minutes.

Chapter 6: Tools for Improving Organizational Skills

Time Management

- Set routines

- Use a timer. Allow the child to wear a watch, not a phone or tablet

- Set a time start and finish for task

- Children diagnosed with ADHD do not have a sense of time.

- Use a digital calendar for weekly planning

- Use a magnetic dry erase whiteboard for daily planning

- Erase tasks, as they are completed, give a reward after all job has been completed promptly

- Use sequence: First. Second, third, last; when competing long tasks

- Eliminate wasting time by setting timers and give rewards for finish tasks before the timer rings. Set a start and finish time.

- Set up on task reminders, a code word, use green cards for on task, red color card as a reminder to get back on duty, or a gentle pat on the shoulder or flicking lights on or off, something quiet and peaceful not a bell or clapping hands.

Establish Follow-Through

- Use the buddy system you are someone else for accountably of an important task

- Set up a homework station, with an area free of distractions

- Supply this area with everything the child will need to finish homework

- Set a timer, set a homework schedule

- Use an on task reminder, (colored card hanging on the wall)

- Give an immediate reward for finishing homework, waiting for the teacher to give a grade

Making Friends

Children diagnosed with ADHD may not have the skills to join a group; at recess, they might try to sit next to the teacher or play alone near the group. They might miss social cues. The best strategy is to model social skills and have children practice and role-play social skills. For smaller, set children play dates. Older children enroll them in afterschool clubs, small group activities at church, community center, or library.

Summary of Training

Explain the training process to the trainee and define expectations, and reinforcements. Next, model, role-play, or create an opportunity for desired behavior. Observe your child naturally (without altering the environment) during daily activities. When the undesired behavior occurs, immediately give a consequence and model the desired action. Refrain from scolding and appearing angry. Only provide a result and re-teach the desired behavior. Use a work that is quick and relates to behavior. A reward should be intangible so that your child will not get the notion that he should be rewarded with things for good behavior.

When giving verbal praise include specifics (ex. You did a good job not screaming when you did not get your way) or, for example, I like when you cleaned your room for the first time, I told you to without whining, good job.

The trainee will become aware that the behavior needs to be changed. Your child will begin correcting the behavior himself or herself.

Every day until the undesired behavior has changed, give reinforcement. Continue close observation as you both go about daily activities. Whenever the desired action is produced, 100% of the training will end, and so does reinforcements. In some cases, after a period of successfully changed behavior, certain situations or environments can cause undesired behavior to reoccur. If this happens quickly, ask the child to demonstrate the desired action or how things could have been handled differently. You do not have to give a consequence, ask the child to come up with a way to avoid the reoccurrence of the undesired behavior. Most importantly, avoid responding to displaying the undesired behavior in anger instead of reacting out of concern and love.

Extracurricular

Extracurricular activities are a chance for the child to direct their energy. Sports help control ADHD symptoms by reducing levels of dopamine and norepinephrine in the brain. Students with ADHD might have to try different activities before what works best for them. Give it some time you will find an activity that your child will enjoy.

- Performing Arts help with cognitive skills

- Hands-on art help with focus

Behavior Strategies for ADHD

- Children diagnosed with ADHD respond better when they are giving a goal to meet.

- Give After...Then, statements that specify what you expect and the consequences. For example, after you complete your homework, then you will get to go outside and play.

- Give a direction and check for understanding.

- Just because the child can repeat what you just said does not mean they can complete the task.

Staying Seated

- Train for extend seating time and sliding down into desk at school using lap weight.

- Require homework to be completed at your kitchen table or a desk.

- Make sure the seat adjusted to the child's height,

- Place a 5lb-10lb bag of rice in a pillowcase

- Lay the rice pillow on the child's lap for about 5 minutes increase up to no more than ten minutes.

After the child has learned to remain seated without the extra weight, discontinue this strategy. This behavior should take about three weeks to train or less.

If staying while completing assignments is not an issue at school, you may need this strategy.

Choosing Schools

When choosing schools, make your observation notes and consider your child's learning style and unique personality. Besides, please take into account your child's behavior as well as his gifts and talents. Search for schools that have support services for action and have a curriculum that matches your child's passions and interests. Furthermore, assure that you think the school's policy for handling behavior issues. Set up an interview with the school beforehand to tour the school and check out the classroom walls' rules and consequences. If possible, get an overall feel of the schools' values and how they handle behavior issues.

Public schools have programs in place for students diagnosed with ADHD, ODD, and CD. Although each district is different, all public schools provide IEP and 504. The upside is that public schools offer sports and extracurricular activities. The downside there is a high teacher-student ratio.

Therapeutic Days schools benefit students diagnosed with CD and ODD. There are schools specifically designed for children diagnosed with behavior disorders such as therapeutic day schools. These schools teach children coping skills and social skills. After the students have learned to produce desired behaviors, they return to their district schools. However, some students may choose to remain for credit recovery purposes.

Private Schools may not offer students diagnosed with behavior disorders; however, they have smaller classes. Students are displaying impulsive behavior benefit from schools that provide lots of activity and freedom of movement. Although they benefit from this type of school for its structure and strict routine, this student may become frustrated and feel anxiety because of intense discipline. The impulsive student and the attention deficit student are to get detention often in this school likely. However, the defiant student may benefit from the structure and strong disciple.

Charter Schools

Charter schools offer IEP and 504's. They also administer the state test. Charter schools are independently run public schools; therefore, each one is different. Again, it is imperative to research the school. One charter school's main focus may be behavior management. At the same time, another charter school's central focus is raising achievement scores. Generally, charter schools have a smaller teacher to student ratio. The attention deficit student may benefit from this type of school because this school may have personalized instruction.

Magnet Schools

The excellent news is magnet schools are specialized in a particular interest that your child might be passionate about. That is a school that may match your child's gifts and skill set. Students with behavior issues may benefit from this type of school because participation boosts self-awareness.

Home School

Home school is an option for students to be free of the restraints of the classroom. It is beneficial for students who need frequent breaks and freedom, like the impulsive or attention-deficit child. Home school a child with defiant or conduct disorders for some time for training purpose and return to regular school after the desired behavior is taught.

Online Virtual School

Most online schools are public schools; most require state testing and IEP and 504 with testing accommodations. The online school is student-paced and may offer personalized instruction and one on one virtual learning. This type of school would benefit the defiant student because he will be in control of his environment. Also, this type of instruction is beneficial to the student diagnosed with ADHD because of the immediate reinforcement after completing each task. However, highly social students may find this type of school challenging.

Chapter 7: Mindfulness Skills for Children and Teens with ADHD

What Exactly Is Mindfulness?

Mindfulness meditation, sometimes called "mindful consciousness" or "mindfulness," is a type of cognitive therapy intended to alleviate tension, encourage self-control, and increase concentration. Caution takes several kinds. It may include relaxation techniques, visualizations, or the disappointingly simplistic act of giving further attention to what you are doing or what is around you.

Most researchers agree that mindfulness could help alleviate the effects of ADHD, such as hyperactivity and inattention, in adults and kids when practiced daily. It may also help relieve everyday tension and the more severe depression and anxiety symptoms that sometimes coexist with ADHD.

Is It Spiritual?

Knowledge is a feature of other faith practices. For starters, Buddhism incorporates a type of meditation on the mindset recognized as Vipassana, whereas some faiths view the act of prayer as a form of therapy.

Yet faith should not automatically be defined as moral or spiritual. It includes paying careful attention to the emotions, feelings, and body experiences in their most simple shape. In other terms, it involves having a better understanding of what occurs to you from minute to minute. Unless you want to, this could be spiritual, but it does have advantages that take place outside any spiritual or religious understandings.

And being mindful works mostly on your brain. It may be utilized as a tool (following adequate medical treatment) to foster their physical health. For managing chronic pain and reducing blood pressure, stress, and anxiety disorders, carefulness techniques were utilized.

How Will Individuals with ADHD Be Improved by Being Mindful?

Mindfulness helps you to give attention, which improves the "concentration muscle" over time. It operates by enhancing an individual's capacity to regulate concentration, self-observe, and establish new attitudes to typically negative interactions. It will even help you more conscious of your emotional condition, and you won't respond too impulsively, often a significant concern for ADHD-persons. However, the issue has still been how individuals with ADHD will use it, primarily hyperactive. However, a new research demonstrates that perhaps the flexibility and versatility of mindfulness allows people with ADHD to fix things for themselves.

Working of Mindfulness Meditation

Practicing conscientious meditation implies paying more attention to the breath, thoughts, and body sensations. It means remaining in the most straightforward way (ideally standing quiet, where you are less likely to get distracted) and concentrating on the air while it moves in or out. As your mind wanders (and the utterly normal phenomenon even for those without ADHD!), just attempt to concentrate on the breathing.

Experts believe that doing this regular exercise for less than 5 mins could help you become more conscious of how one's attention strolls and give you techniques to regulate it in your everyday life. Even before you realize able to concentrate on one's breath for 5 mins at a time, the duration of your guided meditation increases gradually to enhance your endurance.

You should also exercise good feeding (watching out for what you consume and keeping your food concentration while your mind is running around). And you should incorporate deep sleep with certain forms of tension management, such as yoga. For example, careful walking is indeed an option; yoga is another widely known way of integrating mindfulness into better living. Since you feel as if you need a bit more help, meditation techniques can help you cope with a proper mindfulness practice, some of which are freely available online.

It would be best if you still practiced your awareness. Turning on the "culture of mind-awareness" in every moment of the day, even if just for just a few moments, is excellent preparation that can long-term help the brain. You're letting go of your thinking activities and turning your focus to what's occurring in real life in the current moment.

What If I Cannot Concentrate?

It's the essence of the human mind that distracts us. That's why the experts stress that distracting yourself doesn't mean you're "failing." It just implies you're a human being. Mindfulness consciousness is not about sticking with the air; it is about going back to the wind, even though you get interrupted. That's what improves your concentrating capacity, and this concentration on changing the mind enables this approach especially beneficial to those with ADHD.

Who Can Do Mindfulness Meditation?

Almost everyone, of just about any age, might exercise mindfulness.

How Much Does It Cost?

Mindfulness is free and is practicable anywhere. There are brief courses or "mindfulness retreats" at different prices, but these are not required to cultivate a successful mindfulness practice. For starters, it costs $185 for a six-week program at the MARC (Mindful Awareness Research Center) at UCLA. Apps for Meditation, such as Zenytime or Calm, might help create more composition and are usually available free of charge or economical.

Researches About Mindfulness

Meditation work has risen significantly over the years. The core characteristics include:

• Decade-old research, published in the medical journal of Applied School Psychology, discovered that kids with general cognitive deficits after an eight-week meditation practice program reveal significant improvements.

• A little unregulated 2007 research reported in the Journal of Focus Disorders found that "Mindfulness practice is a viable therapy in a subgroup of adolescents and adults with ADHD, and can enhance behavioral and neurological disabilities."

• A recent study has found that carefulness training for both ADHD parents and kids enhanced adherence with kids, resulting in greater overall happiness with home life for kids and parents.

• In 2007, a UCLA group completed a joint-type study involving twenty-five individuals and eight teenagers, half of whom had ADHD. Subjects made substantial gains in both hyperactivity and inattention, increased their performance on cognitive tests, and recorded becoming "less worked out" by the end of the analysis.

To present, eight kinds of research have tested the effect and usefulness of careful instruction in a therapeutic environment for adolescents and adults with ADHD. They have shown positive results in this growing region.

Parents were given proactive leadership instruction in six experiments in conjunction with the kids' mindfulness study. Combining kid care preparation for ADHD for similar diligent parenting instruction appears to be a rational and balanced strategy that approaches both family and adult level ADHD. It would benefit that kids and parents actively demonstrate mindfulness, helping parents better grasp what the infant is experiencing and improve awareness skills.

A new analysis involving eighteen adults with ADHD (Aged between 13 to 18) with their caregivers have utilized the MY mind approach. 4 weeks before the school, on the last and first preparation days, and six weeks following completion, all teenagers and parents filling out surveys. There were no significant improvements in the time before school. Compared to the guardians' scores, kids' inattention, handling conflicts, and peer interaction concerns increased dramatically immediately after instruction. Parents viewed themselves as less anxious and more diligent in their upbringing. These outcomes were maintained during the 6-week aftermath, with further reduction in parental stress. Kids and teens didn't disclose any necessary changes after mentoring, but the 6-week follow-up reported considerably fewer validating issues.

Training of Mindfulness for ADHD

ADHD is marked by inattention, impulsive, and hyperactive actions and is one of the most prevalent behavioral health issues, with 5 percent of kids currently fitting the diagnosis requirements. Medication is now the best and available treatment for ADHD. The last thirty years have witnessed a sharp increase in opioid prescriptions for ADHD, with about 70 percent of kids and teenagers currently seeking treatment being ADHD diagnosed in the USA. However, concerns were raised about limitations of ADHD drugs and their adverse effects, the need for continued utilization to maintain positive impacts, low response to medication, stigma, and unsure long-term efficacy and safety. Therefore, the need for non-pharmacological therapies for ADHD is strong. Still, the effectiveness of those presently accessible, such as nutritional supplements, free supplementation of fatty acids, cognitive therapy, neurofeedback, and therapeutic strategies, is uncertain. There is a need for more approaches addressing main ADHD symptoms.

One revolutionary approach that aims to address critical signs for childhood ADHD is safety preparation. The mindfulness program is based on east meditation practices combined with Western psychological knowledge. It aims to raise awareness by deliberately paying close attention at present, improving considerate observation, and decreasing automatic thoughts.

ADHD in Early Years and Mindfulness

At first glance, ADHD and mindfulness seem to be a contrasting mixture of practicing meditation, and staying still for a prolonged time may sound like an unlikely feat if one has difficulty holding concentration and wants to be busy. However, considering some of the main elements of understanding, it is evident how it would help someone with ADHD suffering. ADHD diagnosed kids are easily swayed by inner and outer stimulation such as emotions and external noises, particularly during tedious or difficult activities, and sometimes forget to shift their focus to what they're doing. During carefulness preparation, kids with ADHD diagnosed are encouraged to concentrate their thoughts on an 'attention source' like their pulse or body, to remain mindful of when to how their focus wanders; sometimes they are overwhelmed by the behavior of other kids, listening or daydreaming to a disturbance in other room. The key to mindfulness is recognizing when someone is sidetracked, being conscious of distraction, and drawing awareness back to the focus. In this way, kids practice their so-called 'attention muscle,' which requires endurance and practice, like physical training, but is likely to increase their ability to control and maintain attention.

ADHD diagnosed kids are often taught during carefulness exercise to evaluate internal and external stimuli that enter their consciousness without functioning on them automatically. It's another critical feature of mindful meditation and tries to target disruptive behavior's primary symptoms. For example, kids can show a propensity to be anxious during yoga, come to their senses out of concern over how many kids have been doing, and blur the responses in answer to the instructor's query WHEN it's not one's turn. These behaviors may also go beyond the reach of a kid; but, by concentrating emphasis on the urges that occur and understanding unconscious trends in their thinking and actions, kids may learn the potential to choose whether to respond rather than responding to triggers immediately. In effect, it can improve their ability to control their irrational and overactive actions during mediation activity and in situations every day. While this can sound rather vague, through playing video games and utilizing examples like the roadway (the quick way to react irrationally) vs the walking route (the faster way to respond with more consideration and foresight), we illustrate this more clearly to kids.

Chapter 8: Working Mindfulness into a Young Life

Knowing When and Where to Meditate

Doing mindfulness meditation as a daily habit is far more comfortable than it may sound at first.

Because mindfulness is all about the individual (in this case, your child or teen), their meditation routine should revolve around their needs.

If school stresses out your young one, then perhaps the best time for meditation is right before they leave for school.

If they start the day strong but accumulate stress throughout the day, perhaps they could take a minute during a break to meditate somewhere quiet, like the library or the office. Arrangements for this can be made with teachers and in a manner that won't embarrass your child or teen.

If your child or teen having trouble falling asleep at night, it would be best to cut TV or electronic devices at least 30 minutes before bed. Those 30 minutes are best spent meditating and calming those thoughts that keep them awake in bed.

You'll quickly learn what areas your young one needs help in and when and where is the best time for them to practice mindfulness.

Many beginners try to master various positions they've seen gurus pose or places they learned in yoga. Tell your young one not to worry about any of that.

It's not about looking or performing a certain way, but about being fully aware of their bodies and minds. Make sure they do it right and do it as they mean it.

Getting Your Child Interested in Meditation

For starters, you need to have your style of meditation. You need to have some sort of practices or routines you can teach your young one.

You wouldn't teach your teen how to drive if you don't force yourself, so how can you teach meditation without being a meditator?

You also need to keep it simple. Don't emphasize "chi" or keywords or Buddhist theology that often comes with meditation groups. You're trying to keep the attention of a child, after all.

Also, don't get too attached to any outcome you've imagined. At first, your child or teen might not even be remotely interested in mindfulness. You can't force them to do it, or else they'll instantly learn to hate what's supposed to help them.

It might even be necessary to bribe your young one.

Maybe your child wants some extra video game time in the evenings, and this could be what motivates them to try meditating with you. With a teenager, you may be able to use the driving time for leverage.

Just remember, there's a massive difference between "bribing" (motivating) your young one and making "an offer they can't refuse." You want them to be motivated to meditate, not to feel like they're being forced.

How to Do Mindfulness Meditation

Mindfulness meditation is easy to do. The first thing your child or teen needs to do is be postured. Here are some simple steps to getting the right posture:

- Have a seat and sit up straight.
- If they're sitting on a chair, make sure their feet are in front

of them and on the floor. If they're sitting on a cushion or mat, they can cross their legs comfortably.

- Keep their back straight. No slouching or leaning back.

- Lay their hands on their knees and slide them slowly up their legs until it doesn't feel like they're reaching anymore.

- Keep their neck straight and head forward, but still relaxed. Too straight, and their jaw tenses up. Too relaxed, and their airway is restricted.

- They can either close their eyes (but keep their ears open) or look at whatever's in front of them.

- Let them calm down and start to take slow, deep breaths.

Those are the basics. Then, we focus on what's going on in your child's mind. I'm talking about the good and the bad.

They need to separate emotions from what's going on "in the now."

What's happening right now and why is it making them feel this way?

What else makes them feel that way?

Teach your young ones to separate the things they can control from the things beyond their control.

Active Mindfulness for Children

Very few children, especially with ADHD, will be excited about sitting still. Usually, their little bodies can't stop because there's so much going on in their always growing minds.

It is your chance to engage their imaginations so they can focus and channel their thoughts and feelings.

Little boys typically like superheroes so that you can take them on a "superhero walk." Taking them for a mindfulness walk exercises both body and mind but in a stress-free way.

You encourage your child to be Batman, Super-Man, Spider-Man, or whatever their favorite superhero may be on this walk. You encourage Spider-Man to use his spider senses and have your son focus on small details around him.

If he's a Superman fan, he'll be using his "X-ray vision" to identify sights, sounds, and smells around them. Batman can keep an eye out for small details where bad guys could be hiding.

If your child is a little girl, she might be inclined to go on a "royal walk" where the princess gets to see, smell, and hear everything in her kingdom.

Your child might also enjoy wandering "off the beaten path" and seeing what there is to see. Maybe there's a smooth, shiny rock in a creek bed that they admire and want to see up close. Have them focus on it and tell you everything they see and feel.

Active Mindfulness for Teens

Your teen may or may not be willing to go on a mindfulness walk with you. It all depends on whether your teen's behavior indicates a need for attention or more independence.

A teenager ought to be old enough and aware enough to identify details in their surroundings without needing to be a superhero.

However, this may be different for pre-teens and younger teens. If your pre-teen is a gamer, he'll be more attentive if you challenge him to find vantage points for enemy snipers and openings where enemy forces could ambush him.

If he's more of an anime fan than a Call of Duty gamer, the same scenario can be translated into spotting openings for enemy samurai, ninjas, and other assassins.

If your pre-teen or young teen is a girl, she might be interested in cheer or dance. How many cartwheels it might take to reach that car parked down the street? How many layers in a cheer pyramid before the top girl can touch that second-story window?

One of the easiest ways to get older teenagers to practice mindfulness is through driving practice. It begins before the car even starts.

Have your teen sit in the driver's seat. What do they see in front of them? What do they see in their rearview mirror? Their side mirrors? What sounds do they hear? and where are those sounds coming from?

These are questions they can continuously go over as they drive on city streets and continually be aware of other drivers and pedestrians. Better yet, a teen that learns mindfulness through safe driving is a teen less likely to be involved in an accident!

Meditation that Works for Your Child

Don't forget that your child or teen's meditation routine may differ from other people's ways.

You can take steps to ensure your young one has quality meditation, and for you to bond with your young one. The best way to do this is to make mindfulness part of your home life.

For starters, set some time aside for family, whether it's reading to your child, working out with your teen, or playing fetch with your dog.

Since the family is supposed to be an essential part of your life, it only makes sense to dedicate time, especially for loved ones.

You might be inquiring what at school is bothering your teenager or what you did to upset your young child. If the answer reveals something that you can control or change, you can meditate on how you'll do it.

It's important to teach your young ones that change is happening all around them.

All people change in little ways over time, both in the way they look and how they behave. Sometimes the change is good, and sometimes the difference isn't so big.

However, don't assume that you know exactly what your young one will say or do. You also need to open your mind if you want to be fully aware of the situation.

Chapter 9: Activities for Children with ADHD

Meditation Activities

You can teach your ADHD child several exercises and practices to help bring the body to relaxation—one of which is breathing. These include traditional meditation and the Chinese martial art of Tai chi. Simply put, meditation is training a mind to relax to focus on other things afterward. The type of meditation you should teach your ADHD child should have its focus on helping your child loosen up, mellow out, and calm down.

Sensory Activities

Poor working memory and forgetfulness are characteristic of children and teens with ADHD. If their attention was not engaged throughout the instruction, they might not remember what the teacher presented. Many people with ADHD also have coexisting learning disabilities, in auditory or visual sequentiality is an excellent means of helping memorize and recall information. Teach and encourage children to create first-letter mnemonics (acronyms and acrostics), which help remember steps in a process or procedure, a sequence of any kind, or other information.

Pair unfamiliar new vocabulary with similar-sounding familiar words

It is called the keyword mnemonic technique, which involves looking for ways items go together (perhaps they say alike or look-alike) to help remember. For example, to remember that

Amsterdam is the Netherlands' capital, one can think of hamsters running around in "Never Land," or the word felons (which sound like melons) can be recalled easily by picturing some melons in prison clothing marching off to jail. Use peg words for learning basic math facts: Three/Tree, Four/ Door, Six/Sticks, Seven/ Heaven, Eight/Gate, Nine/Line. Various programs use the peg word technique and imagery in memorizing and recalling math facts.

Gratitude Activities

There are times you feel like no matter what you do, everything is a struggle for me. You have absolutely no room for error, one mistake, one bad day, one negative comment, one wrong move, and you are done. You're a failure. I just want to matter, I want to be considered, I just want to be included. Sometimes I dream of being invisible. Of not being seen, of not standing out, of not being criticized. Someday I can't take it; I just can't handle the social pressure, the unapproved behavior, the constant judgment, and criticism. But why?

Talk to Them

Tell them you love and appreciate them! Face it, they want to hear it. Even if they've heard it so many times before, tell them you love them. Tell them you appreciate them. Tell them they are working hard. Make sure to have that talk before they leave for school or come back from the day at work. Tell them you love them again and again until they feel like you're really showing them you love them. Find things you can do together. It doesn't have to be anything crazy. Children will be excited about all sorts of things. Try to find things that you can do together that will make the both of you happy. If your child has a special activity they'd like to enjoy with you, big or small, make a point of doing it.

Relish in Their Successes

It doesn't matter how small. Cheer for them it not only shows them that you care, but it's a great way to remind them that they can achieve and improve. It's also an excellent way to remind yourself of the good they do and the progress they make even if they still have a long way to go. Show your children that you care, it's a good way to start changing their lives.

Arithmetic and Counting Activities

Math is challenging for many students and children diagnosed with ADHD. Yet, school districts continue to cut funding for professional learning focused on supporting teachers on math instruction. As the annual calls for STEM innovation echo through our public schools, the continued effort to improve math instruction seems like it would be a common agreement. Some standards must be taught and tested in order to measure learning and performance. However, the limited education of many teachers cannot be an excuse for a lack of effort to improve the way we teach math. Assessments and test scores are not the only benchmarks to consider in a student's understanding.

Here are some suggestions for parents to use and build on. These activities may lead the children to have more creative ideas of their own. If children with ADHD have self-directed learning, they will perform better in school. They also need to know the benefits of their efforts and the benefits of achieving success.

Set goals with your child. Have them write them down and then have them list the steps they need to take to achieve those goals. Have them share these goals with the class or school. Children diagnosed with ADHD often have more difficulty learning math. Parents can help children learn math by encouraging them to try to keep track of their time. There are items such as your watch that can be used for timing. Learning math also includes activities such as measuring, estimating, and problem-solving. Yes, even math is a problem-solving activity.

Children who are diagnosed with ADHD need to feel they are learning. They also need to feel the rewards of success. Provide encouragement and a deadline, but make them know the goal is in reach. Children need to know it is okay to be slightly late and that it is acceptable to go a little bit home or tomorrow. They need to know that there is available help if they need it, but they need to find their own help. Children with ADHD are not stupid and they can work as a team to bring together a solution to a problem.

To become successful, children need to be willing to work, to practice, to follow directions, and to be interested in sports. They need to be able to understand conventional instruction and how it leads to learning.

Answers to some math word problems. You can make a flashcard chart on which you put your answers. While they are learning, self-monitoring can be a great tool to help them understand what they are doing. Children need to experience success in order to feel good about themselves.

If your child has ADHD and is not able to tell you when they are having trouble, take the time to ask them. Children sometimes feel guilty about not being able to solve a problem. Children with ADHD are often smart and their parents are struggling to help them with something that is beyond their ability. It is okay to guide children and help them, but it is not okay for the parents to do the work for them. Teachers must understand that it is not acceptable to penalize children for not completing a work activity. Children who have ADHD still need to be able to participate in the activities. It is okay to allow children with ADHD to use a computer. Computers are more self-directed; there is no teacher correcting everything. They have support from their parents and their home.

Children with ADHD can learn to keep a written record of their time. This is valuable because they are learning to think and to organize the time spent on their work. Having a written record can be of great help. Even if you write just a few words, it can be a powerful help.

Children who are able to solve math problems as outlined above are more likely to get more work. They are more likely to get on the honor roll and more likely to get into gifted classes. They are less likely to be labeled as having a learning disability. But above all, they are more likely to feel good about themselves.

Emotional Awareness Activities

We know that the child having ADHD is hard to read their feelings. It's hard to know how others will react to situations if they never stop to consider how they themselves might react. Here are the tips on how to develop your child skills of emotional awareness.

Tip 1 – What Do Emotions Look Like?

You can buy posters that have all different emotions for the children to color in. Select the emotion you would like, print the poster out, and have the children color the appropriate picture. The children will see the emotion, be able to recognize it from the picture, and be able to choose an emotion they are feeling. The children can then briefly tell you about the emotion they have chosen and why they chose it. An activity like this can also be used to assess whether the children understand the longer guidance session.

Tip 2 – What Do Emotions Feel Like?

Make up a card for each child to fill in, with the emotions they have felt (love, anger, fear, sadness, happy, responsible, confident,), and have them hold up the card to show you. Then have the children express their feelings. You can take the opportunity to mind your feelings. For example, anger is a very natural human emotion because we have all been angry at some point in our lives. This is not a negative emotion; we all have the right to be angry. However, there are different levels of anger, and sometimes anger can turn into something that is not acceptable. If we feel they are not being listened to, or that our opinions are not respected, or we feel unable to change something, or if someone has hurt us that does not make us angry, it makes us upset.

Chapter 10: ADHD Coaching

How Parents Can Help ADHD Child with Organization and Time Management

Raising a kid with ADHD is not like conventional childrearing. Regular rule-making and family patterns can grow to be nearly impossible, based on the form and seriousness of your child's signs, and that means you will want to adopt various approaches. It may get frustrating to deal with a few of the behaviors that result from the child's ADHD; however, there are means to make life simpler.

Parents should take the truth that kids with ADHD possess functionally distinct brains from people of other kids. While kids with ADHD can nevertheless find out what's acceptable and what is not, their disease will make them prone to spontaneous behavior.

Basics of Behavior Management Treatment

There are two basic principles of behavior administration treatment. The very first is rewarding and encouraging good behavior (positive reinforcement). Then eliminating rewards by adhering to lousy behavior with ethical consequences, resulting in the extinguishing of terrible behavior (punishment, even in behaviorist conditions). You instruct your kid to know that actions have impacted by establishing principles and clear results after disobeying these principles. These principles have to be followed in each part of your child's lifestyle. That means in the home, in the classroom, also from the societal arena.

Decide Beforehand Which Behaviors Are Acceptable and Which Aren't

Behavioral alteration aims to help your child think about the effects of activity and restrain the urge to act on it. That requires compassion, patience, affection, power, and intensity on the part of the parent. Parents should first choose which behaviors they will and will not endure. It is essential to adhere to those guidelines. Punishing a behavior daily and letting it another is detrimental to your child's progress. Some actions must remain unacceptable, such as physical outbursts, denial to wake up in the morning, or unwillingness to switch off the TV when advised to do so.

Your son or daughter could have difficulty internalizing and minding your guidelines. Rules must be clean and straightforward, and kids ought to be rewarded for after them. That may be achieved with a points system. By way of instance, allow your kid to accrue points for good behavior, which may be redeemed for spending cash, time in the front of the TV, or even a brand new video game. When you've got a listing of house rules, then write them down and then place them where they are easy to view. Repetition and positive reinforcement also can help your child better understand your principles.

Establish the Principles, But Allow Some Flexibility

It is essential always to reward good behaviors and dissuade harmful ones. However, it would be best if you were not overly strict with your son or daughter. Bear in mind that kids with ADHD might not accommodate to change in addition to others. You have to learn how to enable your child to make errors as they understand. Odd behaviors that are not harmful to your kid or anybody else ought to be approved as a member of your child's human character. It is ultimately detrimental to dissuade a kid's quirky behaviors simply because they believe they are unusual.

Handle Aggression

Aggressive outbursts from kids with ADHD may be a frequent issue. "Time-out" is a very efficient means to calm both you and your child. If your child ends up in people, they need to be instantly eliminated in a serene and critical method. "Time-out" ought to be clarified to the child for a time to cool off and consider the negative behavior they've shown. Attempt to dismiss somewhat disruptive behaviors as a means to allow your kid to discharge her or his pent-up energy. But destructive, violent, or intentionally disruptive conduct contrary to the rules you set should be penalized.

Additional "do not" for dealing with ADHD.

Create an Arrangement

Create a pattern for the child and stick with it daily. Establish rituals about foods, homework, playtime, and maternity. Simple daily activities, like getting your kid to lay out her or his clothing for the following day, can offer fundamental structure.

Break Tasks into Manageable Bits

Consider using massive wall sockets to remind your child of the responsibilities. Color programming activities and assignments may keep your child from getting overwhelmed by everyday activities and college assignments. Even morning patterns should be divided up into different tasks.

Simplify and Organize Your Child's Lifetime

Produce a unique, quiet area for your child to see, do homework, and choose rest in the chaos of daily life. Keep your house tidy and organized for your kid to know where it all goes. That helps decrease unnecessary distractions.

Restrict Distractions

Kids with ADHD welcome readily accessible distractions. Video, video games, along with the pc, promote spontaneous behavior and ought to be controlled. By decreasing the time together with electronic equipment and raising time doing participating tasks outside the house, your child is going to get an outlet for energy.

Boost Exercise

Physical activity burns off excess energy in healthful ways. Additionally, it helps a child focus their attention on particular movements. That can decrease impulsivity. Exercise can also improve concentration, reduce the risk for anxiety and depression, and excite the mind in healthful ways. Most professional athletes have ADHD. Experts think that sports can enable children with ADHD to find an excellent method to concentrate their fire, focus, and energy.

Interrupts Sleep Routines

Bedtime could be strict for children who have ADHD. Deficiency of sleep wreaks inattention, hyperactivity, and recklessness. Helping your child get better sleep is more vital. To help them achieve far better rest, remove stimulants such as caffeine and sugar, and lessen TV time. Set a healthful, relaxing bedtime ritual.

Encourage out-Loud Believing

Kids with ADHD can use deficiency self-control. That induces them to talk and behave before thinking. Consult your child to verbalize their ideas and justification once the impulse to act outside appears. It is essential to know your child's thought process to assist them in suppressing impulsive behaviors.

Boost Wait Period

Another way to restrain the urge to talk before thinking would be to educate your kid on pausing a second before speaking or responding. Invite more thoughtful answers by assisting your child with homework assignments and inquiring interactive queries about a favorite TV show or publication.

Believe in Your Kid

Your child probably does not recognize the strain that their illness might cause. It is essential to stay optimistic and inviting. Respect your child's good behavior so that they understand when something has been done correctly. Your son or daughter will struggle with ADHD today, but it will not continue forever. Get confidence in your child and be more confident in their potential.

Discover Individualized Counseling

You cannot do anything. Locate a therapist to work together with your kid and offer yet another outlet for them. Do not be reluctant to seek out help, should you want it. Many parents have been so focused on their kids; they fail their particular psychological needs. A therapist may help handle your stress in addition to your kid's. Local service groups might also be a beneficial outlet for parents. In addition to visiting clubs and organizations often, attempting to ascertain new ones may enhance the process. It is a good thought to have additional people in the household to cheer them up and help with developmental challenges.

Take Naps

You cannot be inviting 100% of the moment. It is normal to become overwhelmed or frustrated by your youngster. As your little one will have to take breaks while researching, you will want your holidays too. Scheduling lonely time is essential for any parent. Think about choosing a babysitter. Fantastic fracture options comprise:

- Opting to get a stroll
- Visiting the gym
- Using a relaxing tub
- Guard yourself

You cannot assist an impulsive kid if you are aggravated. Kids mimic the behaviors they see them around, so if you stay controlled and composed through an outburst, it will enable your kid to do the same. Make the time to breathe, relax, and gather your thoughts before trying to pacify your son or daughter. The calmer you're, the more relaxed your kid will wind up.

"Don'ts" for Coping with an ADHD Kid

Do Not Sweat the Little Things

Be eager to make some compromises along with your son or daughter. If your kid has accomplished two of those three tasks you delegated, consider being flexible with the following uncompleted job. It is a learning process, and also tiny steps count.

Do Not Get Overwhelmed and Lash Out

Bear in mind your kid's behavior results from disease. ADHD might not be visible on the exterior, but it is a handicap and needs to be handled as such. If there are times you start to feel frustrated or angry, do not forget that your little one cannot "snap out of it" or even "just be ordinary."

Do Not Be Negative

It seems simplistic, but just take things one day at a time and keep in mind to maintain it all in outlook. What's embarrassing or stressful now will fade out tomorrow.

Do Not Allow Your Kid or the Disease Accept Control

Bear in mind that you're the parent, and also, finally, you set the principles for acceptable behavior in your property. Be patient and nurturing, but do not permit yourself to be intimidated or humiliated by your kid's actions.

Growth And Sigh: Morning (And Day) Routines to Reinforce Calm

Getting to school on time demands elite executive acts, time direction, and attention, explaining why your youngster's tardy slips. Find out how comprehensive patterns, bedtime snacks, along with a good alarm clock will help.

The threads. Your kid hops thankfully from the bed. After cleansing her, she heads to the cabinet and picks something out suitable for the entire season. Before her first mouthful of cornflakes, she assesses her back to be sure she's got all her assignments. She then heads into the school bus with five minutes to spare.

Ok. So it is you who is dreaming.

More importantly, your morning starts with you attempting to rouse your kid, who needs nothing more than to be left alone. Fifteen minutes after, once you stop by her room to call her to breakfast, then you discover her consumed in a match, half-dressed. And when she is seated at the desk, she balks at precisely what you are providing for breakfast.

Launch the day may be stressful for any parent, especially for those of us whose kids have attention deficit disorder (ADHD or ADD)—and consequently require the time to begin or can easily be sidetracked. Try out these ideas for starting daily on a much better note.

Long-Term Planning

Establish and examine the morning pattern. Make a graph that details the exact arrangement where every morning action should take place with your child. Help her get in the practice of speaking to this graph daily. (To get pre-readers, use images to denote actions, like a toothpaste ad clipped out of a magazine to signify a teeth-brushing moment.) Or have your child create a tape recording where he informs himself precisely what to do and when to perform it—no longer being nagged by mother or dad!

Chapter 11: Time Management Tips

Please, do not take the tip categories too literally, or you may miss some tips that just might be right for your family. Happy Organizing!

• Show your child a calendar or stopwatch. Instead of saying, we are going to grandma's house the following week, say something like in seven days we are going to grandma and each day, let your child cross a day off the calendar. That will be magnified if you get your child her calendar. If you start this early, you will easily transition your child to a simple planner when ready for school.

• Use a timer when requiring your child to share toys or take turns, preferably using one to see or hear the seconds passing. Your child needs to see time passing because he is so caught up in the moment.

• Before you leave home to go to a fun place with your child (where most likely he is not going to want to leave), think of a routine you will engage in when it is time to leave. It is best if you always have the same way whenever you frequent a place your child is likely not to want to go. Routines are a child's emotional anchor and help him to transition smoothly. In general, children have a difficult time with transitions. Help them along by anticipating the changes before they occur.

• Offer your child another fun alternative when you require them to stop or leave a pleasurable activity. Offer them the enticing experience of an art and craft activity or a favorite treat to motivate them to leave the park cooperatively. Always reward her cooperative behavior.

• Get a large clock timer that will sound when you come into the child's room to wake him up, not entirely depend on you but the clock itself. Eventually, at best, by school-age, he can transition to the alarm clock.

• Post a household routine at your child's eye level so your child can learn how you are structuring his day. Use broad visual cues for your child. A sizeable pictorial schedule works well for young children. Instead of writing breakfast, you might want to post a small picture of toast and eggs or your child's typical breakfast foods.

• Point out to your child how time is measured by having them quickly retrieve an object or get something for you in an allotted amount of time. You may make it a game to see how fast the child can get something for you that has the added benefit of learning to clean up quickly.

• Schedule a family time to clean the house and let your toddler or preschooler clean while viewing the timer. That works incredibly well when assigning him an unpleasant chore. The child begins to see that time is not related to a task's difficulty but its duration.

• Provide incentives to your children who notice a schedule change and cooperate with you. While young children need structure, they also must accept that, at times, their schedules will be interrupted. They have to admit that fact graciously. That fosters respect for time and structure yet builds healthy coping skills.

• Young ADHD children are just beginning to actualize themselves, and they need to understand that time is an entity in and of itself. If you can get them to understand this concept, they are well on their way to mastering their time. Engage them in a conversation using specific time words such as after, never, etc.

School Age 6-9

- Post calendars in kids' rooms, especially early elementary children, with little time when they become the child's personal property to cross off the days until a particular event occurs.

- You can also have your children make calendars themselves monthly or decorate calendars. Get blank calendars from websites or make them yourself. See our list of resources.

- Get your child an organizer/planner and show them how to use it. Many children already have planners but do not know how to use them. The planners must be easy to use and check them regularly until recording in the planner becomes routine or habit for her. The planner must be wide-ruled for young children with a month at a glance and the ability to use their assignments weekly and not just daily. When children only document things every day, they fail to develop big picture thinking. They will also need a practice of you thinking it with them until it becomes a habit. See our list of resources for parents in the appendix.

- Frequently point out to your children that time is measured in seconds, minutes, and hour intervals. Practice jumping jacks (or arm flaps or some equivalent physical action) for one second, one minute, and five minutes. Discuss how you felt doing the same thing for the specified minutes.

- Give your child a fun writing or drawing assignment. (This only works if she likes to draw or write) Call time, once you notice the child is enthralled in the activity. Your child will get frustrated when you call time after only fifteen minutes or so.

- Generally, we concentrate on intervals of fifteen minutes or less. Young children will begin to understand that they must plan their project in a concise amount of time.

- Regularly set the timer to give your child a limited amount of time to perform a creative task or do something in the house. If your child gets frustrated and does not start on the project, discuss what he would have done, and repeat the task frequently. This activity is also great to provide mom or dad a bit of much needed quiet time as it occupies your child. By using this as a springboard to discuss the importance of planning study times realistically.

• Post a household routine in an appropriate view so your child can begin to understand how you are structuring his day. Use broad visual cues for your child and include his school schedule on your planner so he will realize that home and school planning is related.

• Give your children their time clock and assign a non-negotiable bedtime. That is an excellent opportunity for your child to begin to get up for himself and to understand. Along with the privilege of getting up on his own is the responsibility to go to bed early.

• Utilize a family calendar to post dates and events. Thus the child begins to understand the whole family operates under the constraints of time.

• Discuss making a goal with your child. Choose a fun destination like learning to ride a skateboard, and then allow your child to write down everything that must be done to achieve the goal.

• Please encourage your children to make educational goals following the same procedure you would go for fun things they want to do, like riding a skateboard. The child learns anticipating, planning, and making goals can be applied to almost any situation.

• Purchase a sturdy family timer. Place this timer in the center of the family dinner table every evening. Ask the child to use the timer to clock "12 minutes!" at the end of each day. In these twelve minutes, he/she can answer questions, make a to-do list of tasks for the following day, or enjoy quiet family time. Make sure the child sees you using the timer every evening.

• Use a flow chart like a drawn racetrack so your child can

visually mark his progress in a task. I once used a racetrack with young children to show them they were progressing towards their reading goals. They advanced the car with each step they made towards their reading goals.

Tweens 9-12

• Place hobby or interest related calendars in your tween's room. They will use anything they can personally relate to because the calendars have your child's interests.

• Assign a summer study project or family research. It should be something that is fun but requires minimal research. Show your child how to use the time grid and study plan to complete the project.

• Encourage your child to make a to-do list for special projects. Ask them to estimate the time it will take to complete each task. You can do this by only taking a big sheet of paper and writing down the top three things you have to do to accomplish the project. Use index cards to record everything, and then have your child put them in sequential order.

• Assign a child to be Family Organizer for the week. This child can check to make sure the whole family is complying with order and organization rules. For instance, she might check to see if everyone is doing his or her chores. That is an excellent job for a middle child who often does not get the chance to take the lead or be influential in family decisions. Many families will consent to the family baby or listen to a dominating oldest, but this allows a middle child to shine.

• Rotate the responsibility of family time and organization manager between siblings or between you and your child weekly. The family time manager gets to post things on the family calendar and remind the family of appointments. We learn best by doing and giving your child the responsibility to monitor his/her time, and the families will do wonders for her self-esteem.

• Assign the task to your child of doing a project such as cooking a portion of the holiday meal. Show your child how to break the job down into sequential steps and how much time is needed to complete each step. You are teaching goal setting that is timed steps to progress.

• Ask your child what she likes to do when she is an adult, then have her research the steps to get there. It will also be helpful if she knows you will work with her to achieve her goals.

• Please encourage your child to record personal and school activities in her planner so that she begins to understand time management involves her personal and school life.

• Read a bibliography of a famous person as a child. Encourage your child to see how the person had successful traits that were visible even when she was a child. That gives your child a vision for his future.

PART II: Preparing Your Child Self-Care Healthy Habits for Child ADHD

Chapter 12: Strategies for the Home Environment

Learning Self-Care

One of the first steps of dealing with ADHD is teaching your child how to care for themselves. As parents, you will be taking care of your child, but when your child knows how to take care of themselves, it is better than that because slowly, they will learn how to be self-reliant. And with that, children who have ADHD also learn how to follow through and stay on track.

You must teach your child not to depend on your verbal instructions alone but to do things independently. That will help them gain autonomy, but simultaneously, they also need to indulge in some self-care. You also have to try and foster enthusiasm about the things that they love in life. One widespread example is making your child learn how to listen to an alarm clock to wake up and not depend only on their mother's voice. But you also have to show your faith and your love in your children and show them that they are worth believing in. No matter what happens, you cannot give up on the child. Whether it is about pouring their juice in the glass or applying toothpaste on the toothbrush, every small task can be accomplished if they have the right support.

Stress on the Advantages

When I am talking about self-care, you probably might be conjuring up some luxurious thoughts, but that is not what self-care is all about. It can be practiced in your way. It can be a set of practical actions made, especially for the well-being of your ADHD child.

If you want your child to have the best self-care, you have to urge them to figure out what they want. When ADHD children are not permitted to look after themselves or engage in self-care, they become even more exhausted, depressed, emotionally depleted, or even angry. When you teach your child how to put him or her on the top of their priority list, they will stop feeling overwhelmed and undeserving. Yes, at times, your teenage child might think that they will start looking after themselves once everything becomes okay, but that can become a far-fetched dream. You need to put yourself first now and teach your kids to do the same.

But there are cases when the children move farther away from their parents when asked to become self-sustainable. That is because children with ADHD always need someone by them, and when you ask them to start learning to do their things, they fear that you will abandon them. They have this risk of rejection in their heads that can be toxic and prevents them from adopting a self-sufficient lifestyle.

You have to make them understand the different advantages of self-reliance. Give them some examples like—when they become self-reliant, they can visit many places, and they can complete tasks even when someone is not present to help them out. The main idea is that you have to make the child realize there is more good to being self-reliant than the bad. You must be careful with the tone of voice and word usage because an ADHD child can easily be affected. After everything you say, see how your child is reacting—whether it is positive or negative. If it's positive, then you will know that you are doing it the right way. You can also keep a note of your child's willingness to become self-reliant and the self-growth that he/she is showing every day so that you can track how far you have come with teaching them self-care.

Practice Color-Coding

The strategy you can use to help your ADHD child work on his/her organizational skills is color-coding. Indeed, ADHD children will face some academic challenges, but that doesn't give them any excuse for giving up on stuff. Color coding is one such strategy that has always helped others who have ADHD to learn things quickly. You can separate the different subjects in your planner in different colors. That will help you understand stuff with just a single glance at your planner.

One way of implementing color coding is to suppose your child has Math homework, and you have assigned the color yellow to math. Then, make sure they put some yellow labels where they are doing the task and make them wear a yellow bracelet to school so that they don't forget that they had math homework and that they have completed it. The bracelet helps a lot because it serves to be a visual reminder of the task. Once the teacher checks the assignment, the child can then take the bracelet off and put it in their bag.

To take things a bit further, then make folders for each subject and label them in a specific color. Organizational skills are made quite strong with color-coding, and your child will be able to follow through quickly.

Pets Can Be Implemented to Teach Being Responsible

When a child has ADHD, pets can do wonders for them. Pets can help to bring a sense of routine and responsibility for the child. That is because pets bring in a burst of positivity at once. You can get your child anything whenever they want—be it a cat, dog, or even a rabbit. Whatever the pet is, you have to give your child the responsibility of feeding the pet and take them out for walks if applicable. Your child will try their best to maintain the responsability because they love the pet, and taking care of them gives them back an equal amount of love.

Moreover, getting a pet like a dog or a cat is even better because even if your child forgets to feed them once, the pet will keep reminding them some way or the other about providing. Animals have their ways of making things understand. Also, when you gift your ADHD child with a pet, it will make them feel responsible. Sometimes, a little amount of motivation or push is all a student needs to get going.

Encourage Good Hygiene

Children who are presently suffering from ADHD face difficulties in doing even the simplest things in life, including maintaining proper hygiene. From the outside, it might feel that your child is not brushing teeth or taking a shower daily, but they think many things on the inside. Being a parent to a child having ADHD is hard, but you have to take it one day at a time and take the baby steps necessary for teaching your child how to take care of their hygiene. Kids who have ADHD frequently get stuck in one particular thought, moment, or activity, and it takes them a lot of time to get done with something.

You might be telling your child a thousand times to shower or brush their teeth, and yet they keep forgetting because this is not how you should teach good personal hygiene values. If you are the person who is always telling them what to do and what not to do, then there will be a point of time where they will not be able to function until and unless you are present with them. Moreover, when you keep nagging with the same things, some children can hate it because it acts as a constant reminder that you doubt their abilities.

When you agonize too much about your child's poor hygiene, they might like that attention and keep doing intentionally so that you give all your attention to them.

One of the factors that aids in the resistance shown by ADHD kids towards personal hygiene are the use of negative words in parents' case. Any form of negativity can work against the well-being of your ADHD child. When you continuously check on your child to make sure they have brushed their teeth or washed their hands, they will see these usual activities negatively as if they are some unpleasant activities. Your word usage should be complimenting the child, and they should be encouraging him/her to maintain proper hygiene. They should not display even a shred of doubt in their abilities.

To let your child brush teeth regularly, you can make a subtle recommendation that dentists always advise you to brush teeth regularly; otherwise, you will get cavities. It is better if you did not ask them to do anything. Sometimes remarks like these are enough to make an ADHD child do a task. Also, you can teach your child how to brush or floss correctly. That will encourage them to do it correctly as well. It would be best to tell your child how great they look when they have brushed their teeth because of a whiter smile.

Some parents keep aiming for perfection even if their child is doing an activity. Don't do that. Let your child brush his/her teeth. Take it one step at a time. If you keep pestering on the fact that the brushing was not right, they might not brush at all. So, don't stress about being perfect with everything.

Help Them to Develop Routines

There is no such perfect or imperfect way to raise a child who is suffering from ADHD. But it is also important when it comes to parenting is that you should instill a structured environment for your child, and they should be introduced to the concept of routines. The first question that you are probably having is how a structure is going to help your child.

Why Is Routine Important?

Whenever we discuss the right way to bring up a child with ADHD, you will often come across the term structure. Do you know what it refers to? It is an environment that is more predictable and organized. To bring the form to your child's life, you have to create a schedule for them and make routines for their day-to-day life. Your child should clearly understand the consequences, expectations, and rules so that their environment is predictable. That, in turn, helps them in feeling secure. The ability to regulate themselves is something that ADHD kids do not possess. They have so many distractions, and staying concentrated on any particular thing becomes impossible for them.

With the presence of a way, completing simple tasks will no longer seem like a burden to the child. They will learn how to set some time out for things like taking a shower, brushing their teeth, or doing their homework. In simpler terms, with these routines, you will teach some good habits to your kids.

Chapter 13: Strategies for Maintaining Physical Health

Movement and Exercise

That will give you and your child a wide variety of options to choose from. It will also allow you to select activities to improve specific ADHD symptoms.

Outdoor Activities

Individual Sports

Your child may find team sports challenging because of his ADHS symptoms, so you might want to consider individual sport instead of helping your child succeed better.

If your child is a sports lover, he has dozens of exciting and enjoyable individual sports to choose from, such as:

- Martial arts
- Tennis
- Wrestling
- Swimming
- Bowling
- Fencing
- Table tennis
- Skateboarding
- Roller-skating

- Ice skating

- Track and field

Your child's natural high energy and enthusiasm will help him succeed in these types of sports and even become a champion!

If your child shows an interest in an individual sport and wants to take classes, a good idea is to take him to observe a class before signing up.

Don't force it! If your child realizes that he's not enjoying a sport he has chosen, don't pressure him into continuing and tell him that he "will learn to enjoy it when he gets better." You may be right, but pressuring your child will most likely make him dislike it more. Children with ADHD have a higher tendency to be passionate about something for a while but then lose interest.

Likewise, if you feel that your child's abilities are perfect for a particular sport, again, don't pressure him if the sport isn't appealing to him. Let your child suggest and choose.

Whatever individual sport your child chooses to practice, it will be a perfect outlet for his energy. IT will help keep ADHD symptoms in control, help him focus better, develop social skills, and sleep better.

Indoor Activities

When the weather doesn't allow for outdoor activities, you need to have various indoor activities to keep your child occupied and give him an outlet for his energy. Ideally, indoor activities should follow these basic rules:

Indoor activities for kids with ADHD need to be: Structured

Kids with ADHD crave structure. They need to know what will follow, what to expect, and how they are supposed to act in each situation.

What will I do? Where will I be? What is okay for me to say or do?

You need to provide that structure for them in the form of structured activities. That means telling your child what he has to do, providing the required materials, and making it clear what he needs to do to win or succeed. An example is telling the child to color in a whole page of a coloring book using three colors.

Indoor activities should involve as many senses as possible. In the above example, you have engaged the child's sense of touch and sight.

Multi-sensory activities help the child focus better. Some multisensory activities include:

- Cooking
- Board games
- Card games
- Building with Legos
- Hula hooping
- Coloring and painting
- Play Dough
- Twister
- Jumping rope
- Balloon volleyball

Indoor activities should involve movement. Of course, this is not always possible with all games. Gauge your child's energy and mood and decided whether you need to structure-activity with more (or less) movement. Or, combine activities with more dancing activities, with quieter activities like board games or video games. Remember to structure time for these activities as well.

Indoor activities can be group activities or individual activities and activities with more movement and quieter ones. Here are some more suggestions:

- Hide and Seek
- Dancing
- Charades
- Baking cookies
- Building
- Listening to audiobooks
- Crafts
- Scavenger hunts
- Singing
- Obstacle course
- Tramp lining

Now that you get the idea, go ahead and come up with some activities of your own to ensure that your child stays active and engaged on those rainy days!

Play Therapy

Play therapy is a fantastic tool. It is used in many psychotherapy and child psychology areas to help children with disorders develop skills while having fun.

You may choose to have your child engage in play therapy with a specialized child psychologist; however, you can easily use this method with your child at home as well.

Art Therapy

This type of therapy helps children develop their creative talents and express themselves through art. The child is asked to make a painting or drawing, describe their day at school, or an enjoyable event, something they like, or even draw themselves as they feel.

The child's artwork may uncover specific issues that he is having, allowing parents or the therapist to discuss them further. Besides, it's just a great way to keep the child focused while explores and develops his creativity and uniqueness. Here are some suggestions:

- Making a collage with old photos or pictures from magazines.

- Designing a postcard with a short message to someone the child is angry with or wants to thank.

- Making a digital slide show with photos that make the child happy (or sad)

- Responding to music; listening to a short piece of music and drawing how it makes the child feel.

- Decorate a window with window markers

- Write a message to a balloon and send it flying away.

- Finger painting

- Drawing a self-portrait

- Making a drawing for someone special

- Drawing with eyes closed

Play Therapy Games and Activities

Experts believe that parents can help children with ADHD make great gains through simple and inexpensive play therapy techniques. Even conventional games like Clue and Let's Go Fish are equally beneficial.

Depending on your child's age and the specific area you want to help him with, you may consider the following options.

Fantasy Play (Ages 4-6)

Children with ADHD often have trouble expressing and channeling their emotions. Fantasy play is crucial for teaching kids with ADHD how to express themselves better when feeling angry or frustrated.

How to structure play therapy?

Set fixed times. Play sessions should be between 10 to 15 minutes so that the child does not get bored; however, if the child retains an interest in the game for longer than that, allowing him to continue.

Prompt the child as he is playing. For example, if you are playing with a puppet named Fred, start the game by saying, "One day as Fred was walking to school..." or "Once upon a time, there was..." During the game, you can also prompt your child by playing a role in the game.

Encourage good social behavior during the game. For example, "What will happen if the doctor shouts at the sick person?" or "How will the little girl feel if her friend doesn't want to share?"

Some suggestions die fantasy play are:

- Playing with dolls
- Doctor kits
- Han and finger puppets
- Stuffed animals
- Action figures and monster figures

Learning Life Skills (6-10)

These skills are crucial to developing at this age as they will remain with your child for life. They include learning to handle frustration and anger, wait their turn, and finish assigned tasks. Games that help build social skills include:

- Let's Go Fish
- The Memory Game
- Chutes and Ladders
- Chinese Checkers
- Clue
- Role-playing with costumes or masks
- Playing with action figures
- Mock tea parties
- Play therapy for older kids
- Strategy video games
- Time management video games
- Superhero role play
- Art therapy

The Science behind Brain Games

Brain Games

Researchers from Kennesaw State University and Augusta State University in the U.S. have shown that brain games can be a new form of ADHD therapy. Brain games stimulate the prefrontal cortex of the brain and help ADHD children overcome distractions. The study suggested that brain games could be an alternative to medication. Following studies have concluded that brain games work to develop the brain, improve focus and attention, and help ADHD kids learn better. The ongoing research is very promising.

Following these findings, dozens of "brain training" programs have emerged, many of them making huge claims that are not backed up by science. My advice is to beware of these programs and stick to traditional brain games like puzzles, riddles, and brain teasers. Do not shell out money to a bogus program.

Brain games benefit children with ADHD by:

- Strengthening memory

- Developing problem-solving skills.

- Enhancing logical thinking and deduction skills

- Improving concentration

- Promoting pattern recognition

- Video brain games that improve visual perception and spatial recognition.

- Enhancing cognitive skills.

- Enhancing reasoning skills.

Brain games help children learn these skills by having fun, which is always the best way to learn. Therefore, it makes total sense to schedule these types of games into your child's activities.

Here are some good suggestions:

- Brainteaser eBooks.

- Brainteaser websites

- Riddle eBooks

- Video brain games

- Crossword puzzle books

- Logic problem books

- Brain game apps. There is variety to choose from suitable for all ages.

- Additional activities and fun games

- Coloring books

Coloring books have been around since our grandparents' time and are generally overlooked in today's digital era. However, the benefits of coloring for your ADHD child should not be ignored. Children are never too old to color, and in fact, paint has been shown to relieve stress in adults! The benefits include:

- Preparing preschoolers for school
- Improving motor skills
- Developing good handwriting
- Enhancing creativity
- Developing awareness of colors
- Improving focus
- Improving hand-eye coordination
- Enhancing confidence when kids are praised for their work.
- Developing self-expression skills.

Music

While most activities are performed with either the left or right side of the brain, music engages both sides of the brain, strengthening your child's ability to multitask.

If your child is musically gifted, encourage him by signing him up for lessons, investing in the instrument of his choice, or whatever else he needs to pursue his passion. Singing groups, orchestras, and choirs are also an excellent way for your child to improve social skills and make like-minded friends.

Drama

If your child loves to act and has the talent, drama groups and classes will benefit him immensely. He will have to focus on memorizing lines and learning to interact with others in a group effort within a structured environment. To top it all off, the applause at the end of the show is just the kind of praise and encouragement he needs!

Debate Teams

That could be a very fun learning experience for your teen. It will sharpen his communication and social skills, challenge his intellect, and showcase his natural enthusiasm and passion. It can also lower his stress level and bring out his best self. Join a local, state, or national debate team. The majority of debate programs are student-run and student-operated. As a team, they will have to follow the debate rules. They are familiar with making directed speeches to a large audience. They write and share their prepared speeches. They are used to being creative and are sometimes even artistic in their speech delivery and argument style.

Chapter 14: Meditation and Breathing Exercise for ADHD

Medication and therapy are good ways to control the symptoms of ADHD. However, they aren't the only options. Research now demonstrates breathing exercise, where you continuously observe your thoughts and emotions may also be a practical way to relax the brain and improve your concentration. According to a 2017 study, one-third of people, especially adults with ADHD, adopt this method, and about 40% give it a high ranking.

Unlike other treatments, mindful meditation doesn't need a prescription or a visit to the therapist's office. You can practice it while sitting or walking, and even with some Pilates.

How It Works

Each time a muscle is weak, you can do exercises to strengthen it, and the same goes for the mind. Mind breathing reinforces your ability to sustain your attention. It explains how to stay focused on something. Moreover, it trains you to bring back and gather your thoughts when you realize you have been distracted. It could also make you more aware of your feelings, so you're less likely to act on impulse.

Mediation is known to aid ADHD because it gives the child a way to deal with their emotions and manage them. If children can learn to control their feelings when they are young, then the lessons will stick with them for life. Therapies like mediation are closely tied to ADHD because it is a psychological disorder. One of the main symptoms is a lack of control over emotions and often leads to acting without thinking. Mediation sessions with children with ADHD may be similar to the 'think box' where the child has to do a task in a certain amount of time and receive a gentle reminder when they reach the limit they have set themselves.

Research asserts that mindful meditation can help relieve the symptoms of ADHD. One UCLA researcher discovered that people with ADHD who visit a mind yoga session once weekly for 2 and 1/2 hours, then complete a regular home yoga breathing exercise that continuously increased from 5 to quarter-hour over eight weeks, were better able to stay devoted to tasks. They were also less overtaken by stress. Other studies after that showed the same results.

Yoga has been shown to help improve ADHD symptoms, especially hyperactivity, impulsivity, and inattention, and maybe as effective as medication for ADHD. Numerous studies have shown that yoga helps regulate the amygdala, prefrontal cortex, thalamus, and other central parts of the brain related to ADHD, restoring normal functioning. Children and teens with ADHD who practice yoga consistently show significant improvements in their focus, cognition, mood, behavior, and sense of well-being.

Other Benefits

Asides from helping people to understand and manage their symptoms, this technique may also help individuals who have ADHD:

- Boost self-esteem
- Reduce stress
- Lose weight

Because individuals who have ADHD have difficulty getting stuff done promptly and may be forgetful, they tend to be very critical. Nevertheless, it would be best if you used breathing exercises as an instrument to tune out the judgmental thoughts in your head.

People who regularly do mindful yoga have been found to have fewer stress hormones when they're in stressful situations, like if you are feeling helpless or uncontrollable.

Research also demonstrates that mindful meditation can lead to weight loss, probably because it encourages you to carefully check out everything you will be doing, including your food.

Options for Meditating with ADHD

Are so many things running through your mind? Imagine a blue sky with fluffy white clouds. The sky represents your consciousness; the clouds symbolize your ideas. Focus on the days of "space" in the middle of your clouds to redirect yourself.

When you have trouble staying still, practicing breathing exercise as you stroll can be just as good as when you're seated. Whenever your brain wanders, gently bring your attention back to the current emotions and reality.

What's the Best Exercise to Regulate the Symptoms of ADHD?

Likely, you have heard that regular exercise can help boost your mood in the right way. When you have ADHD, exercising can help you feel good, and it's also a vital way to control your symptoms.

Whether you are watching a session of kung fu, taekwondo, or you are in the middle of a self-defense course, you will indeed find yourself immersed with much of your attention to the movements of your feet and legs. Glancing at your opponent's hands and arms will only happen occasionally because there is so much to be focused on in the lower part of your body. However, for people with ADHD, they are more attentive to non-lower parts of the body, which can be essential to exercise regularly and stay tuned to the ADHD well-regulated symptoms less intense.

To get these rewards, you need to understand when to pull the breaks and when not to. The essential thing is to identify and understand what exercise suits and interests you best and then be consistent.

Get the Most out of Active

The results of exercise may last for long, precisely like medicine. So, consider your workout as a remedy, "drugs." Aim for at least 30 to 40 minutes of exercise each day, 4 or 5 times weekly. The training you choose is your choice, but ensures to keep the activities moderate while exercising, because:

- Your heartbeat increases

- You begin to breathe hard and fast.

- You sweat

- Muscle tissue feels tired.

Consult your doctor if you're unsure of what kind of exercising technique to adopt. She may recommend a heart rate monitor or several others to ascertain that the workout wasn't futile.

Types of Exercise You Can Do

Aerobic Exercise

This is whatever gets you pounding. You must do something that boosts your heartbeat and maintain it for about thirty minutes to forty minutes.

Aerobic exercise creates new pathways in the mind and floods it with chemicals that help you to concentrate.

You can any of the following:

- Running

- Walking hurriedly

- Biking

- Swimming.

You can do these activities outdoor or indoors, but when you have a choice, go out. Studies show that being outdoor when you exercise can lessen your ADHD symptoms more than when you exercise inside.

Fighting Techniques

Experts assert that the more technical your exercise is, the better it is for the mind. When you undertake fighting lessons, you will be trained in skills like:

- Concentration
- Balance
- Timing
- Memory

If knowing about fighting techniques isn't your thing, alternative activities that can also help the brain and body are:

- Rock climbing
- Dance
- Gymnastics.
- Yoga.

Strength Training

If you're just getting started with exercise, choose aerobic activities like walking or running at first. Once you've been at it for quite a while, then other types for variety.

Try exercises like:

- Lunges
- Squats
- Pushups

- Pull-ups
- Weightlifting.

Team Sports

If you join a softball or little soccer league, they must help you stay up and fit. Organized athletics has the advantages of exercise using the added reward of the interpersonal group to motivate you.

Teamwork hones your communication skills and will help you think about your actions and plan. Being one of the team may also improve your self-esteem.

How to Keep at It

The same as medicine, exercise might help you treat ADHD if you keep cycling or doing whatever technique you've adopted. However, if you have difficulty concentrating, how do you want to keep up with the course? Try the following tips:

- Hold it interesting: You can stay from the rut if you change your activity each day or weekly.

- Have a friend: A workout buddy can help you stay on track, and at the time you sweat.

- Exercise in the morning: If it fits into your program, training should be the first thing every morning before taking your drugs. That way, you'll have the most remarkable excess mood-boosting chemicals in you.

Chapter 15: Strategies for Maintaining Spiritual and Mental Wellness

How Spirituality Helps ADHD Symptoms

- It helps your organization

An individual's spirituality helps them connect to a higher and more profound sense of purpose and state. Spirituality enables you to find order amid chaos and maintain organization. Lack of proper organization is a known issue and symptom exhibited by individuals diagnosed with ADHD.

Another problem that individuals with ADHD have to often contend with is lack of or inadequate system. Spirituality and spiritual exercises provide you with a framework and guideline to manage life's chaos when faced with life's day-to-day confusion. The spiritual life of an individual gives him or her a mission. Something to live for. Therefore, he or she would strive to fulfill this mission and, in this way, put order into an otherwise very haphazard disordered life.

For example, belonging to a particular religious organization like a church helps you work toward fitting into that organization structure like attending services, praying daily, reading the Bible, and singing hymns. The practice of everyday rituals offered by the religion you belong to in collaboration with the group provides a structure that helps ADHD individuals see life in a more organized and focused design.

Spiritual exercises like prayer, thoughtful meditation, reading the Bible, songs of praise and worship to God provide the soul with a deep sense of relief, a calm and a calmness that makes him or her lay aside the cares of the world and become much more focused.

Verses from God's word can support a family that has to contend with the symptoms of ADHD. For example, stories of Biblical characters like David, Ruth, and Esther can serve as a source of inspiration and provide you with the audacity and bravery needed to go through difficult conditions, especially when you suffer from people misunderstanding you, as is usually the case in the lives of individuals with ADHD.

Faith in God takes your soul beyond the state or position where the mind and body cannot reach. Trusting that God loves you even when you are suffering and that He has a particular purpose for you will provide you with a lot of comforts when inundated with feelings of confusion and are downcast in spirit.

Faith in God makes you continuously move and work with the notion that you are specially made and unique before God and man. It helps you to understand that everything works together for good in the life of those who love God, including people who have ADHD. It would help you to see your ADHD problem as a means to an end. Rather than view your symptoms as an obstacle, you tend to view them as tools to help you get to where you need to be. This thought would help you learn how to manage it better and much more appropriately.

Faith in God and prayer gives a child with ADHD, the inner grace and patience needed to cope and deal with the symptoms of ADHD.

Evidence of the Connection Between Spirituality and ADHD

Neil Nedley, M.D., demonstrated in his study and book "Proof Positive" that spirituality and trust in God play a significant role in the healing and treating a lot of common diseases. The study also demonstrated how spirituality could boost the health and quality of life of an individual in addition to the quality of life of those closest to him or her. In an enthralling study that looked at Americans' religious experience, which reached 100 years of age, it was discovered that their involvement in religiosity significantly boosted their physical health. The benefits of their trust in God goes beyond just attending religious services.

Apart from enhancing people's well-being, religious practices, and faith go beyond age and racial boundaries. Another study of African Americans discovered that individuals who engaged in organized religious activities improved their lives and gained more satisfaction. Those who engaged in religious practices outside a collective structure also experienced some boost in their state of well-being and happiness.

A significant finding across many different racial groups showed that the practice of spirituality is a great benefit to one's quality of life. This benefit in the quality of life brought about by engagement in spiritual exercises is exemplified in the research titled "Faith in God Favors Good Health" and provided by a Duke University researcher.

The benefit of spirituality is contagious. It does not only benefit the individual in question but other members of the community, including non-believers. Research has also shown that communities as a whole are healthier when more people in that community demonstrate a life that is built on trust in God and a life that emphasizes implicit obedience to God and his standards of conduct: the Ten Commandments.

Non-believers also benefit from their neighbors' spirituality because social norms favor traditional values to the healthier lifestyle embarked upon by their neighbors who engage in spiritual activities. After an individual undergoes a comprehensive "historical and physical" examination with suitable lab or other essential medical tests, the doctor using the result obtained can typically give a distinct image of the patient's health status. The health status generally determines what the individual frequently feels and experiences as the quality of life in a day to day living. This health status is just only a part of the whole essence of the person's being. Other reasons are much more significant to the point in question. Furthermore, individual health status is directly connected to their habits. Take, for example, a person who has formed the habit of eating red meat. The more red meat he eats, the greater the amount of cholesterol in his system and the higher his likelihood of suffering from blood pressure, heart disease, cancer, digestive issues, concentration issues, renal failure, and renal health issues.

Although this is true, there are a few exceptions where an individual is brought up in an environment favoring a heavy red meat eater. A particular culture that an individual grew up in dramatically determines the individual's habits when he grows up. However, there are cases where an individual grew up eating red meat and whose parents are smokers and drinkers, yet the individual does not smoke, does not drink, and is a vegetarian. Such an individual chose to work against the already existing culture and start to practice different habits and allowed his personal choices and values to take precedence over the culture he was brought up.

Finally, every individual's personal choices are due to much more than the prevalent culture. Therefore, an individual's options and personal values are very much connected and depended on his overall sense of meaning and purpose in life.

There is an overall sense of being and purpose in life directly related to the individual's spirituality and trust in God. This illustration thus shows that belief in God has positive implications for health. That same trust directly affects the individual's overall meaning and purpose, which affects his or her values and choices. Thus, personal values and preferences affect the culture they choose to adopt, which directly influences the specific set of healthy habits that directly impacts their health and total state of well-being. Trust in God, therefore, builds health entirely and makes it stronger.

The majority of physicians aware of this eternal truth try to integrate this healing aspect in their medical practice to restore their patients to normal health. Thus, it is significant for a holistic cure to be accurate to incorporate the spiritual element into the diagnoses and treatment procedure. Trust in God is a good treatment option for ADHD symptoms and the right way to prevent ADHD. When children are brought up with Godly values and a strong sense of wellbeing from their early life stage, it curbs their possible tendency to these abnormal behaviors and symptoms.

Some children have a tendency towards ADHD, but through the proper emphasis on their Biological, Psychological, Social, and Spiritual life, it can be significantly helped and even cured.

Chapter 16: Peaceful Parenting: Mindfulness Tactics for Parental Stress Management

N ow that you are utterly energized from all the mindful movement and physical ideas we will present some peaceful parenting tactics to employ more self-care and holistic health in your lives and roles. When working with or parenting a child, tween, or teen with any diagnosis, especially ADHD, we often undergo real feelings of immense pressures, marital strife, physical and mental health struggles, time and financial management, guilt, anger, sadness, loss, frustrations, stress, blame, and other adult challenges.

As mentioned, mindfulness is not a magical cure or pill to swallow, but it can undoubtedly melt away stress and anxiety, like the Wicked Witch of the West was dissolved by the water in the movie. Once you master the basics and accrue practice over time, you will see the results in yourself and your kids! Experiment today with at least one of these Grateful 8 Strategies. They are not listed in any particular order of importance, so feel free to mix and match:

• Under the Sea: Whether you are a wondrous water baby or a lovely landlubber parent, it is necessary to deeply and truly connect with your inner parental mermaid/merman and maintain a parenting model that is not all about perfection.

Keep yourself afloat and your head above the waters. Recognize that like water freely flowing, parenting a child with ADHD is not stagnant and a perpetually picture-perfect or pretty pond.

Ride and let the waves and whirlpool of colorful emotions and evolving learning experiences exhilarate you and unveil your inner strengths amid the serious struggles (and sharks!). Do not forget to play and splish splash along with the way because humor will be your life vest as you surf steadily in life, teaching, coaching, and parenting!

- Love Lingo: This technique is also imperative. Use your words, mindfully and compassionately. Do not fight fire with fire; do not allow comments to become weapons when parenting kids, tweens, and teens with ADHD. Of course, this does not mean that you must speak in eloquent poetry and poise all the time but learn love lingo.

Why? It can tenderly tame your tongue when we use love lingo instead. Following suggestions from Conscious Parenting experts, I have learned to take a moment literally since we as parents must really try and discern the difference between reacting to kids with ADHD from the central state of who they are and our own proud, parental egotistical worlds.

While this advice might sound a bit harsh, love lingo roots us in reality and empathy, so it affirms that we as adults have already had our own time to grow up and learn the ropes of this world. Thus, love lingo is powerful because it reminds us not to make it all about us adults. What does this mean? It does not encourage you to be a pushover or doormat, but try not to take everything personally, although I know it is much easier said than done.

It also forces us to stop comparing ourselves to other parents, the Kardashians, and everyone else out there. Who cares what others think about us as parents and people? Be authentic and live in love with your skin! You are not in a pageant or parenting competition, so learn love lingo for confidence and empowerment.

One way to employ better love vocabulary is to have some handy dandy one-liners when tensions are high to diffuse your adult egos. My favorite one, for example, is "I love you too much to argue." It works like a charm with my kids, spouse, and family members. What will be your love lingo line/lines be? Think creatively and practice, practice, practice. Live the love vocabulary when you are "Livin La Vida Loca!"

• Pregnant Pause: No, this strategy is not advocating a plan to conceive another bun in the oven, foster an entire football team, or adopt triplets, but I assure you that it is one of the easiest ways to integrate mindfulness into your daily life routines and parenting approaches. Simply add a pregnant pause and breathe deeply when you feel overwhelmed, frazzled, angry, or ready to give up. Newport's (2018) article in The Magazine for Addiction Professionals offers an idea from the legendary guru, Thich Nhat Hanh, who advises us to stop and truly take a moment to envision or recite this mantra, "Breathing in I calm my body, breathing out I smile."

I love this idea so much that I suggest repeating it based on your age (or your kiddo's ages): so if you're 40, does it forty times! Words are so powerful, so "word up" with this holistic wisdom to cope with ADHD!

• Slow Your Roll: Of course, you can order some yummy sushi when you are overly stressed and over the parental edge, but this conservative strategy is equally imperative. Reduce and slow your pace as a family and parent. In general, Race & Piquet (2015) assert how our kids today are sadly growing up "in a culture that constantly stimulates the stress response—fight, flight, or freeze" Take a moment tonight and look at your calendars objectively.

Kids with ADHD can become overwhelmed so quickly and over-stimulated. Don't let tons of back to back, crammed scheduled events, technologies, or rushing around everyday exacerbate the ADHD triggers. In turn, slow your roll, you'll! Take a minute and critically reflect upon this week's calendar. Talk to your kiddos about which ones to prioritize. Discuss together ones to possibly modify or delete to spend more face time with your kiddos, not Facetime, the app. Slow your roll before stress takes a toll!

• Balancing Act: Parenting mindfully does not mean being

a cop or being a lenient buddy to kids 24/7. In actuality, it is genuinely about respectfully setting limits and reinforcing your authority with "I'm the adult here." It does not always feel this way when parenting, so this helpful tip is one of my favorite pieces of advice for adults.

Similarly, the article "Wonder Years" from Essence helps us realize that as early as nine months, we must model and reinforce to children consistently which behaviors are acceptable and those that are not. If we are constantly frazzled and depressed when dealing with a kid's diagnosis, then we automatically model the negativity and toxic vibes that follow.

Think like a gymnast and find that proper balance; center yourself holistically and mindfully as a parent to keep your stress minimized and your confidence flying high amid ADHD!

- Chillax: Taking a timeout is not just for kids. In reality, adults equitably need to take breaks to remain grounded and sane when parenting, coaching, mentoring, or treating kids with ADHD in any capacity or role. Suppose your child is having a major meltdown, tantrum, diva session, or rebel without a cause chaos moment. In that case, I suggest using this technique on yourself called "Stop, breath, and chill," as Francis (2008) advises in "Peaceful Parenting" from Scholastic Parent and Child.

When attempting to take my daughters today to lunch at Panera Bread, I sat with them on a small couch in the middle of a crowded mall while I was trying to order online, so we could skip the line and go straight to our table. I asked them to play calmly with their sticker books together while I typed. In less than 30 seconds, a circus ensued: they rambunctiously used the public couch as a trampoline, started pulling each other's hair, kicking, pinching, and sobbing loudly. I then had to apply this technique to calm myself first before attending to their mall mania literally. When do you need to chillax the most as a parent? What are you currently doing to destress less?

Along the same lines, this super strategy is heralded by many other psychological and educational experts. Again, Francis (2008) contended that "Once you've reached a place of acceptance", add some positive self-talk to swap "I'm going to snap!" with "I've got this!" Ready to chillax? What will be your self-talk phrases? Write them down now and start practicing, please.

• Bookworm: Do not stop learning as an adult. Learn from resources, books, other parents and experts, etc. Arrange playdates with other families to share ideas. Find parenting books at your local library, on Kindle, or listen to a mindful podcast or webinar about positive parenting. Bookworm it, baby! Some of my most enlightening parenting tips come from parenting blogs because the writers are enveloped in the trenches daily.

• Pump It Up: Exercise is essential and something that parents need to maintain mindfulness, health, and sanity. I know many experts recommend striving for roughly 10,000 steps per day, but my personal goal is 7500. If you lack the time or funds to join a public exercise class or facility, I keep loving the convenience and effectiveness of these online ones that I can do while my kiddos nap.

I swear I am not receiving any promotional or monetary compensation for suggesting them. They have toned and changed my life and mental health. They are also free and readily adaptable to suit any level of need. Pump it up for parental patience and power in whatever way suits your style and preference.

Chapter 17: Nutrition and ADD

Today, more doctors and parents turn to nutrition rather than medication to alleviate symptoms of ADHD in children. Parents prefer more natural options while doctors fear the adverse reaction of drugs.

Research has shown that there is a close relationship between ADHD symptoms and nutrition.

Two necessary studies in Holland concluded that eliminating foods like gluten sugar, processed meat, food dyes, eggs, and dairy products improved ADHD symptoms in 70% of the children participating in the study.

Another study was published in the Journal of Attention Disorders in 2010. It showed that the typical "western diet" high in protein, fat, and sugar doubled the risk of ADHD.

Another study published in Pediatrics in 2010 concluded that certain pesticides found in fruits and vegetables might cause ADHD and heighten ADHD symptoms. The study recommended organic produce as the best option.

Many more studies have proven the relation between nutrition and brain function.

Basic Nutrition Facts

• Studies show that protein boost awareness, whereas carbohydrates increase sluggishness of the brain and body, thus decreasing alertness.

• Sugar makes ADHD symptoms, mainly hyperactivity, worse.

• Food additives and artificial coloring aggravate ADHD symptoms

The bottom line is: An ideal diet for a child with ADHD is rich in protein and vitamins, low in carbohydrates and sugar.

How Nutrition Affects the ADHD Brain

• Brain cells require adequate nutrition to function optimally.

• Myelin, a substance that sheaths brain nerves and cells, dopamine and serotonin, two hormones that modulate brain function, play a significant role in heightening or decreasing ADHD symptoms. They can be maintained and balanced with certain foods.

• Serotonin is essential for balancing the mood and regulating sleep.

• Dopamine promotes focus and alertness and increases motivation.

• Proteins affect brain function by providing an amino acid that produces neurotransmitters. The better neurotransmitters are nourished, the better they perform, delivering messages to the brain cells.

• A protein-rich breakfast and lunch are an excellent way to keep the ADHD brain focused and alert at school and throughout the day. Doctors have also reported that this diet type may reduce the discomfort and side effects if the child is taking medication.

• The right diet can affect your child's mood, cognitive function, memory, and behavior by promoting his brain function.

Nutrition Rules for Your ADHD Child

• Monitor impulsive eating. The hyperactivity and impulsiveness associated with ADHD may drive your child to eat impulsively, leading to unhealthy weight gain. Schedule mealtimes and snack times and try to limit your child's eating between meals.

- Give your child lean, high-quality proteins. That includes organically-raised poultry, organic eggs, wild fish, and grass-fed beef. A high-protein breakfast will make a big difference in the child's ability to focus throughout the day.

Your child should eat some form of protein daily in moderate amounts as too much can also be unhealthy.

- Give your child healthy carbs. Carbohydrates are an essential part of any diet. But replacing unhealthy, simple carbs with complex ones will not aggravate ADHD symptoms. Healthy carbs include whole-wheat products such as bread and pasta. Vegetables and fruits are high in fiber, like apples, yams, and blueberries.

- Beware of sugar. High amounts of sugar induce hyperactivity and restlessness in all kids. Allow your child moderate amounts, and whenever you can, use natural sweeteners in food, such as honey and fruit juices.

- Remind your child to drink plenty of water. Dehydration impairs the brain's ability to function optimally and to focus.

- Healthy fats are great brain foods. At the top of the list is Omega-3, which is a great brain nutrient as it boosts concentration and memory. Omega-3 is found in most types of fish and avocadoes, lean grass-fed beef, and leafy green vegetables. Serve fish once or twice a week to keep your child's brain alert and better able to retain learning.

- Get creative with herbs and spices. Studies have shown that certain spices and herbs are great nutrients for the brain. For example, turmeric, which is found in curry and saffron, eliminates the buildup of plaque in the brain and is a potent antidepressant. Cinnamon improves attention, while thyme, sage, and rosemary improve memory.

- Monitor your child. Not all children with ADHD will have the same reactions to food. That is why you need to monitor your child to see if certain foods heighten ADHD symptoms. Eliminate or limit such foods from your child's diet. The most common foods reported aggravating ADHD symptoms are gluten, high-fat dairy products, energy drinks, soda, and candy.

Best "Brain Foods" for Your Child

The following foods are great brain boosters in general. Be sure to include them in your child's diet, and over time, you will see an improvement. The list of foods is too extensive to have here, but kids generally like the following foods:

Apples and Pears

They are an excellent source of complex carbohydrates. Give your child an apple or pear before bed to improve his sleep.

Eggs

A great source of protein which is essential for a child with ADHD. Try to give your child organic eggs.

Blueberries

Besides being packed with antioxidants, blueberries help boost communication between brain cells.

Whole Grains

A great source of carbs that will help keep your child's brain focused and alert. Whole grains include brown rice, wild rice, whole-wheat pasta, whole wheat bread, and legumes.

Avocadoes

They are rich in protein and omega-3 fatty acids, improving blood flow to the brain, and promoting focus and concentration.

Broccoli

Not all kids are crazy about broccoli, but it's packed with vitamin K. Studies have shown that people who consume higher amounts of vitamin K in their diets have better memory and focus. If your kid hates it, try to "hide" it in others by whipping it into fruit shakes or sauces.

Tuna

Most kids love tuna. There are many ways to incorporate them into different dishes, such as salads, wraps, and casseroles. Tuna is packed with Omega-3 fatty acids, known to improve ADHD symptoms, especially memory and retention information.

Bananas

They are packed with fiber and are known to have a calming effect.

Raisins and Dried Fruit

Studies have shown that they improve memory and focus.

Turkey

A great source of lean protein and contains an amino acid called tyrosine, which promotes brain health

Worst Brain Foods for Your Child

The following foods have been found to trigger or increase ADHD symptoms and should be avoided.

• Gluten: Studies have shown that gluten aggravates symptoms in people who have ADHD. To be on the safe side, eliminate gluten from your child's diet.

• Artificial sweeteners and food dyes

• Deli meats

• Caffeine

• Frozen fruits and vegetables may trigger ADHD symptoms. Fresh is always better for your child and the whole family.

• Saturated fats such as fried food, pizza, and fast food

• Soda drinks

• Candy. Candy is loaded with both sugar and food coloring, a disastrous combination for kids with ADHD. Avoid it as much as possible.

• Sugared cereals

• Cake mixes and frostings, which are high in sugar and contain food coloring and artificial flavoring.

Suggestions for Healthy Snacks

Kids love to snack, and this is where problems can occur when kinds of snack on unhealthy foods packed with sugar, bad carbs, and saturated fats. Encourage your child to snack healthily by offering the following snacks, packed with protein and fiber, to help calm ADHD symptoms.

A Fruit Salad or Fruit Shakes

That is a snack no kid will turn down, especially when topped with a scoop of low-fat drone yogurt instead of ice cream. All fresh fruits are packed with vitamins and minerals and promote brain health.

Peanut Butter and Jelly

This combination is an excellent source of protein and fiber. Just make sure that you use low-sugar or sugar-free jelly and serve the snack on whole-wheat bread instead of white bread.

Mixed Nuts

Another good source of protein and healthy fats, especially walnuts.

Healthy Mini Pizzas

That is a filling snack that your child will love. Use whole wheat muffin halves for the base and top with cheese, fresh tomatoes, herbs, or any other topping your child loves.

Feta or Goat's Cheese on Toasted Pita Bread

Another filling snack to give your child an excellent protein and fiber boost.

Whole Wheat Crackers or Pretzels

That is an excellent alternative to chips, cheese puffs, and similar snacks that trigger hyperactivity.

ADHD and Food Allergies

Some children with ADHD may have adverse reactions to certain foods such as soy, milk, corn, grapes, chocolate, and oranges. Monitor your child to see if he has any sensitivity towards these foods and if they trigger symptoms.

It may come as a surprise that food can significantly affect your ADHD child or how crucial proper nutrition is. Now, you are armed with another great tool to help your child control ADHD symptoms and have better brain health.

If you try to reduce the effects of ADHD on your child with traditional therapies, you will reduce the negative effects of food as well. When a child with ADHD eats a balanced meal, the proper nutrients go straight to the brain and support his ADHD treatment.

After a while, your child's ADHD medication will work better too. No matter what ADHD treatment you use, remember that nutrition is the cornerstone for good health. Good nutrition will ultimately help your child reduce ADHD symptoms and have a better brain.

PART III: ADHD and Relationships

Chapter 18: Life at Home and Beyond

Impact of ADHD on the Daily Life of a Child

Symptoms of ADHD are inattention, hyperactivity, and impulsiveness. As parents of children with ADHD already know, these three symptoms are just the tip of the iceberg. Almost every part of the child's life is affected by ADHD. The social, emotional, and academic impacts are present not just when the child is at home but also in school, at friends' houses, at restaurants, family vacations, and many other places (or at least they will be as soon as the child enters adolescence). As adults, these children become job-seekers and employees. Their social lives change from lively to, well, nonexistent. Their academic or career success is limited, and they become limited in many other activities, from sports to hobbies to volunteer groups. At home, they even become limited to a small room, as they can no longer deal with the disorder and its symptoms. The child faces problems such as forgetfulness and disorganization, not only at school but also at home.

Impact of ADHD at School

Although children with ADHD face problems at school, it's not that they are not intelligent. They have an IQ equivalent to the students without ADHD.

Children with ADHD face problems in learning, yet ADHD cannot be termed as a learning disability. Children with ADHD also have indicated a higher probability of learning disabilities affecting math and reading majorly. As many as 50% of children with ADHD have been found by research to be affected by at least one learning disability.

Students with ADHD face significant problems—They are disorganized and forgetful. They lose items now and then. Often they find it challenging to keep track of projects, remember homework assignments and tests. They also face problems keeping track of all the essential information needed to manage their studies.

The primary symptom of ADHD is inattention. Instead of focusing on one task, the ADHD student is often distracted by the stream of sensory input coming in.

Sitting still through class is a massive challenge because of hyperactivity. Passage of time would expect students to acquire maturity, and also, an increased ability to remain seated through discourses is required. However, hyperactivity is a sticky problem and doesn't go away as quickly—continuing to be a heightened challenge over the school years.

Impact of ADHD on Family Life of a Child

Parents often find it challenging and taxing to have an ADHD child as they need more attention and care. Parents often end up supervising their homework and assignments for hours. As the child cannot complete the given tasks with due responsibility, parents find themselves more involved in these tasks such as assignments, projects, or homework. Making sure that their child completes these chores in the given time becomes taxing at times. It is also necessary that both parents pitch in and work together. If they are unable to do so, they find they are arguing with each other unnecessarily. Often parents end up thinking their partner's behavior with the child is not right. He/she is either harsher or more lenient when not required. In such circumstances, it becomes tough to have a peaceful family life. It is also observed that families are torn apart due to this problem.

Parents are not able to devote an equal amount of time to other normal children. Also, children with ADHD often quarrel with their siblings as a result of their impulsive behavior. They act without thinking and fight with their siblings. That makes the siblings feel neglected so much that they resent the attention given to the ADHD child. Parents also feel guilty about the attention given to one child and lack of awareness to another.

ADHD children cannot follow typical disciplinary methods and hence parents need to find new techniques. Raising these children will become a lot easier if the system of rewards and consequences is followed. For example, if the child completes the work in time and follows instructions, reward him with something he can't resist and vice versa.

The parents may feel exhausted and tired due to their continuous monitoring and the time they spent getting the projects and assignments done. Parents have their dreams of a calm and peaceful family life. But their priorities need to change for the sake of the child. The ADHD child is their top priority now.

ADHD is a hereditary disease, and there is a fat chance that one of the parents has ADHD, and then it is a challenging situation to handle. That can play havoc in day-to-day life and lead to unstable parenting and a chaotic household.

The parents getting diagnosed with ADHD after going through the diagnostic process with their children are familiar.

If one of the children is with ADHD, the home can never be tension-free. The parents always find it challenging to cope with the situation and are often tired, frustrated, and tense and feel they can't take it anymore.

Impact of ADHD on Social Skills

Children with both ADD and ADHD face difficulties making friends.

ADD children are shy and reserved. Being introverts, they have a tough time making friends. But if they make friends, they stick to them and remain friends. At the same time, children with ADHD are impulsive and hyperactive. On the surface, they may appear friendly, extroverted, and energetic. They may easily reach out to other children, but they cannot maintain friendship due to their impulsive nature.

Children with ADD or ADHD often lack emotional maturity. Comparatively, their classmates could be emotionally mature, stable, and years ahead of them. That makes it difficult for children with ADHD to relate and connect with children their age.

Research has also established that children with ADHD, who suffer from emotional outbursts or behave aggressively, have trouble being in harmony with their peers. Many children with ADHD feel "different." They feel as though they do not belong there. They can feel lonely. They also may feel embarrassed and disgraced if they are criticized either by the teacher or their friends.

ADHD children benefit by doing activities in small structured environments. Activities such as Boy Scouts or Girl Scouts, hobby classes, extracurricular activities such as music, dramatics, martial arts, sports, and fine arts like craft and painting are beneficial. These activities provide ADHD children an opportunity to mingle with other children while they are being supervised.

Emotional Problems

As a rule, people develop emotional maturity until the age of 35. In ADHD people, this requires more time than ordinary people. Say, for example, a person with ADHD may need at least seven to ten years extra to reach a level of emotional maturity of a 21-year-old. In the case of children with ADHD, it is observed that their emotional maturity level is well below that of their non-ADHD peers.

Low self-esteem is another trait found in ADHD people. Struggling years in school or the feeling of being inadequate aggravates these feelings. This feeling of low self-esteem is also observed in ADHD adults as ADHD children who were not diagnosed or treated in childhood often bring these feelings of low self-esteem when they grow up.

Also, anxiety, depression, bipolar disorder, and learning disabilities are commonly found in ADHD children. That complicates diagnosis and treatment.

Chapter 19: Other Practical Tips for Helping Your Child Cope with the Demands of Daily Living

A child with ADHD struggles through day-to-day tasks that other children seem to breeze through. You can help your child cope better by following these practical tips:

Create Structure

Your child will find it easier to focus, concentrate, and complete tasks when doing them in expected places and at scheduled times. He needs predictability, familiarity, and structure.

Create this structure at home and sustain it. When your child is familiar with the situation and knows exactly what he is expected to do, he is more likely to do better.

Establish a Routine

Create rituals for play, homework, meals, and bed. Make them simple and predictable.

For instance, teach him to prepare the things he needs for school before he goes to bed. Have him put them in a specific place. When he wakes up in the morning, he is less likely to experience anxiety. He knows his things are ready. He knows where they are.

Help Him Keep Track of Time

Use clocks. Put a big one in his room. Use alarms. They serve to remind him about the things that he has to do at particular times.

Simplify His Schedule

Do not expect too much from your child. Consider his abilities with the particular demands of the activities you want him to participate in.

If you get him to commit to more than what he can handle, he may become too distracted, nervous, and "wound up"—and become ineffective.

Give him enough time to finish assigned tasks so that he does not panic or give up.

Use Charts

Charts are useful visual reminders for tasks your child is supposed to do—daily chores, homework, special assignments, and the like. If it is a big task, break it down into smaller chunks so that your child does not feel overwhelmed.

Make the chart fun and attractive. Use colour codes. Decorate it with stars or points for good behaviour.

Make Checklists

If your child finds any task (usually a multi-step one) stressful or complicated, a checklist will serve as a memory aid to help him feel in control and organized.

For instance, make a list of all the things he has to have for any school day and tape that checklist on his door.

Use Timers

A child with ADHD has a short attention span. He gets antsy when he has to concentrate on what seems to him an extended period.

Deal with this issue by setting a timer for 15 or 20 minutes every time he has to do homework. When the timer rings, your child can take a short break, after which he sets the timer again for another 15 minutes.

Your child will not get bored or give up when he knows he can enjoy a mini-break after every quarter of an hour. Doing homework will seem more tolerable.

Create a Quiet and Private Space He Feels Comfortable in

Your child will be better able to focus on his homework if he has a cool, comfy, and quiet place to work in.

Keep Your Home Tidy and Organized

A child with ADHD struggles to be organized. Set a good example by keeping your home neat and organized. Your child will feel more at ease when he knows exactly where to find the things he needs.

Establish Rules for Your Home

Let your child know that you expect him to follow specific rules and expectations. Make the rules clear, simple, and easy to understand.

Remind him of these rules by writing them down on a large sheet of paper. Tack the sheet of paper on a wall so your child can easily refer to it anytime he needs to.

Set up a simple system of rewards and consequences. Sit down with your child and discuss what will happen when he obeys or disobeys the rules.

Be consistent. Stick to what you say. Follow through with a reward or consequence as agreed upon.

Keep Your Child from Situations that Are Too Difficult for Him to Handle

Your child may react in a volatile manner when you expose him to a situation that he is not emotionally ready for.

If you know that he quickly gets impatient and edgy, do not make him endure long waits. If he usually bursts into a temper tantrum when he does not get what he wants, do not take him with you to a store where the array of toys is likely to overwhelm him.

Encourage Him to Verbalize What He Feels When He Is Upset

Finding the words to express his feelings will slow him down. It will temper the need to act out. It also makes him realize that when he takes the time to think about and express his feelings aloud, he can better curb impulsive behaviour.

Use Timeouts

You can use a timeout as an appropriate consequence for inappropriate behaviour. It is a firm, relatively brief, and acceptable way to instil discipline.

A timeout interrupts your child's out-of-control behaviour. It defuses it and allows your child to regain control. It is the right way of teaching your child to accept the results of the action he has opted for.

Help Him Make Friends

Children with ADHD are often easy targets for teasing. They talk too much, say inappropriate things, interrupt repeatedly, can't read social cues, and often come across as either indifferent or too intense or aggressive.

On the other hand, many kids with ADHD are brilliant and wise. Left on their own, most can figure out how to make friends with the right kids. Moreover, some children are likely to find their "quaint" ways quite charming and funny.

That being said, it is always good to help your child learn social rules and skills.

Sit down with your child and tell him gently but frankly about his unique challenges. Suggest ways for him to make changes.

Teach him how to become a better listener. Teach him cues, so he knows how to read body language and facial expressions. Teach him how to interact more easily with his peers.

Role-play with him. Imagine a range of social scenarios that he is likely to face. Switch roles. Make exercise fun.

Help him befriend kids who have similar physical skills and language, so he feels comfortable with them. When you invite his friends over, begin by inviting only one or two. Be at close range when they play. Do not tolerate any form of bullying, yelling, pushing, or hitting.

Give him space and time to enjoy the play. Reinforce good play behaviour with a smile or praise.

Show Him that You Love Him

Your child needs to know that you appreciate and love him. When you focus only on correcting his inappropriate behaviour, you may end up hurting your relationship. He may feel unloved, undeserving, and unappreciated. His self-esteem may suffer even more.

Look for Ways to Increase His Self-Esteem

All kids have unique talents and interests that parents should foster.

Every small success helps to build a child's self-esteem. A

child with ADHD often does well with martial arts classes, music lessons, or art projects. Find out what your child is interested in. Find out what he is good at. Then look for an activity he is likely to enjoy and excel in.

Be Generous with Praise

Children who have ADHD are often rebuked for their behaviour. They frequently receive complaints, corrections, and criticism for almost everything they do or don't do.

Do things differently. Hold back the negative comments. Give more positive reinforcement. Be generous with praise.

Focus on your child's appropriate behaviours rather than on the inappropriate ones. Give a smile or a positive comment every time he completes a task, no matter how small. Give him small rewards for small accomplishments. Keep in mind that what comes easy for another child may be pretty tricky for a child with ADHD. Praise him for his effort.

Encouraging Thinking Out Loud But Also Promoting Waiting Their Turn

You may be wondering why on earth, anyone would be recommending that a child with ADHD be encouraged to think out loud. Is that not one of the biggest problems you are facing? Indeed, children with ADHD will often say things out of turn or act without permission, which causes rifts in their environments and settings such as school or public spaces. When your child is in one of these settings or even at home, they have a particular set of instructions that they are supposed to adhere to. Whenever they speak or act out of turn, they typically do not follow that instruction and are landing themselves in trouble. So far, we are on the same page. However, thinking out loud is a little different. Because your child acts or speaks impulsively, you have seen it frequently land them in trouble. However, by encouraging them to think out loud, you can get a better sense of your child's thought process and can, therefore, help them control their impulsivity. They are learning to wait their turn before speaking is an essential skill that can be taught alongside thinking aloud.

Once you and your child have worked on moderating their impulsivity, you can begin to teach the skill of learning to wait their turn, which is essential for the rest of their life. As you are most likely well aware, children with ADHD lack self-control. As a result, often they are acting, speaking, jumping, dancing, throwing things, and everything else under the sun before thinking through their possible consequences.

Children with ADHD rarely can process their thoughts or actions before speaking or acting on them. It is these actions of interrupting or knocking over supplies that most likely earn results in numerous behavioural write-ups in your child's take-home folder and a rapidly declining conduct grade. Learning to think through consequences is an essential skill that your child will need to adapt to be successful students and eventually competent adults. To understand this skill, one technique is to encourage thinking out loud.

When your child is encouraged to think out loud, it means that you are stopping them before they interrupt or misbehave, and you ask them to walk you through their thought process to tell you why they would do what they were about to do. For instance, if they are about to throw a toy at their sibling, you will stop them before this happens and ask them why they thought throwing a toy was an appropriate response to the frustration that they were feeling. You might ask, "What did your sibling do to make you angry?" Your child may not be able to answer this right away, which is where your help comes in. Try to help them find the words to communicate the emotion that they're feeling. A particular feeling prompts the action of throwing. Perhaps that emotion is anger, frustration, sadness, dejection, or even embarrassment. Your child is probably already aware of some of these emotions, but it's your job now to connect the action they were going to take with the emotion they felt to analyze what they were feeling and learn how to address that emotion better.

Chapter 20: How Each Executive Function Affects Home Organization

Flexible Thinking

What is the executive function of flexible thinking?

Flexible thinking allows you to move freely from one situation to another and adjust to respond appropriately to each case.

In other words, to go with the flow.

Both ADHD and anxiety impact flexible thinking. It's not uncommon for people with either diagnosis to have a rigid "my way or the highway" response to change. It is my experience that this is often a reaction to the loss of control.

What just flashed through your mind?

Were you excited?

Frustrated?

For how long?

There is no "perfect amount of flexibility." Flexible thinking is all about how easily you can pivot and deal with the unexpected life throws at you every day.

In addition to helping you adjust to day-to-day changes in your schedule, flexible thinking affects how you view spaces in your home and what labels you put on different types of containers.

Here is why you need flexible thinking to get your home organized.

When you have robust and flexible thinking, it means that you can adjust to the unexpected.

You roll with the punches.

You can go with the flow.

You can pivot.

If you do not have flexible thinking, you're very rigid. You want to have a very structured day; you don't like it when unexpected things happen. One minor thing can occur in the morning, and your entire day will be off.

Now obviously, no one is entirely flexible or completely rigid. That is a spectrum, too, right?

I am pretty flexible, and I can think outside of the box to come up with solutions. But when unexpected things happen, it does knock me off my game for a couple of minutes.

If any unexpected events happen in a row, then maybe it will derail half my day. Sometimes it will derail my whole day. Everyone has a threshold of how many things can come at them unexpectedly without throwing them completely off course.

Here is an excellent example of what I see happen 99 percent of the time when I come in as a professional organizer to work with a client who does not have flexible thinking.

They have tried organization, and it has not worked.

They think: "Okay, I'm ready to get organized." In their minds, "get organized" equals:

Go to Target and go to the area where they sell organizational supplies.

Pick out a whole lot of plastic containers with lids, in whatever color I like.

Spend a couple of hundred dollars on those.

Bring those home to whatever area of the house is "unorganized."

Put all of my stuff into these beautiful containers.

Put the containers on the shelves.

Put a picture on Facebook.

I'm organized.

Then what happens is, it doesn't work for them.

They can't remember what they put in the boxes.

They can't remember to put stuff back in the boxes.

They buy more stuff because they forgot what box they put it in.

They didn't buy clear boxes, and they can't see what's in there.

So they resign themselves to failure. "Great, I tried that whole organizational thing. I spent a good $200 and three days of my life to organize my pantry. Then I had to go buy a bunch of new food because, by the time I found where I had put my old food, it was all expired."

You might be laughing, and you might be thinking: "Bingo. That's me. And that's why I hate organization, and I can't be organized."

Not true.

The organization has nothing to do with containers. You've just been sold that bill of goods.

Often, if you don't have flexible thinking, what you think is that this one solution solves this one problem, and if it didn't work for me, that problem can't be solved for me.

Somebody with flexible thinking can see more than one solution to your problem.

Problem: You want your pantry to look like Pinterest. You are tired of seeing empty boxes that have no cereal bars in them. You think you have cereal bars for the kids. You get up in the morning; you go to the box, it's empty. Kids have no cereal bars; you're frustrated; somebody has to organize this pantry. Right?

Solution: I hang over-the-door shoe pockets on the back of my client's pantry doors. I cut them in half, so they only cover the bottom of the door and hang them with Command Hooks. Then you can see all the different kinds of cereal bars and protein bars and protein shake mixes that you have at one time.

The pockets are small enough that 5 to 10 bars will fit in each bag. It's low enough that the kids can get their snacks. It's easy enough that the whole family can follow the pattern that you've set out. And then, when you plan to go to the grocery store, you can look and see which cereal bars are most popular and which ones you need to buy again.

This system works well when you're on a new diet, and you're trying all these different flavors of protein bars. You can have all the other flavors in various pockets and easily see at the end of the week that everybody in the family liked most because that's the empty pocket.

Different Solutions for Different Problems

The organization is done in incremental stages.

If you went and bought a hundred dollars' worth of beautiful plastic containers for your pantry, it probably worked for at least 50 percent of your foods. The bins for grains of rice and starches may be working great.

Then, you tried the cereal bars organizer on the door, and that is working. But you haven't found the right solution for the cereal.

Now you are in organization level two, where flexible thinking is hard.

Problem: What is another way I could organize cereal? Emptying all the grain into expensive Tupperware containers with lids didn't work because the kids didn't put the covers correctly, and all the cereal went terrible. (Guess how I know this doesn't work.)

Solution: What I've started doing with all of the clients I organize is just taking all the bagged cereal out of the box. Then, we put a chip clip on the bag and put all the cereal bags in a basket.

All cereal comes in a clear bag inside its box. When you pull that bag out of the box, you can see exactly what kind of grain it is through the bag. It works with Pops Cereal and Apple Chex and all of them. They all look different, and they're all in clear bags. That works fabulously. It takes up less space than those expensive containers do, and you can roll the bags down tighter, and the cereal stays pretty fresh.

Now we've solved your cereal problem. There's only one problem with this cereal solution: What if you buy both Honey Nut and regular Cheerios? They look the same without the cardboard packaging. So you need to take a Sharpie marker and write on the bags which is which. Other than that, this has worked for everyone that I have organized cereal for in the last five years.

Now, if you struggle with flexible thinking, what's going to happen is that because you don't understand these different systems, you are thinking, well, okay, great. You told me where to put cereal bars, and you told me where to put starches and cereal. But you didn't tell me where to put tomato soup. And because you don't have flexible thinking, you don't know what to do with your soup. I didn't even mention a canned item. What do you do with canned soups?

That is why flexible thinking impacts your organization skills. You do have to be kind of relaxed when you're organizing. Try different things. Keep what is working and try other solutions for what is not.

Match the Container to the Stuff

Here's another example of flexible thinking. I was organizing my nightstand drawer. And my nightstand drawer has office supplies because I sit on my bed and do my work at night.

Problem: I had bought different drawer organizers for my nightstand drawer in the past, but they weren't working for the items I was currently storing. The traditional desk-drawer-organizer storage compartments were too square. I needed thin rectangles.

I went and bought a few drawer organizers, and I brought them home. They didn't work at all.

Solution: I went back to the store. I went up and down every single aisle, looking at every single organizer that would fit in that drawer, and thinking about the things that I had to organize.

- A 7-day-a-week pill container
- Pens and pencils
- Nail polish supplies
- ChapStick
- Mints
- TV remotes

I looked all over the store—in the bathroom supply aisles and the kitchen supply area, not just the office supply area. Anything that was plastic and would fit in that drawer, I looked at.

I ended up coming home with an acrylic utensil holder that you would put in your kitchen to organize your silverware drawer. And to be honest, I would not buy this one for the kitchen because unless you only have four spoons, it wouldn't be big enough. But it was perfect for my nightstand drawer.

Chapter 21: Life at School

Developing the Desire to Achieve

Your son will stuff his schoolwork into his backpack as if it were trash, depending on you to sift through his documents, uncover his teacher's notes, and find assignments. It's "out of sight, out of mind" for him. You end up telling him of all the stuff he's not completed yet. He tells you that he's going to do it later but never comes later. You press him to do this, and he does all he can to squirm free.

So what can you do to help your child overcome its guilt, alienation, and social acceptability concerns? Which strategy would allow him individually complete schoolwork and enjoy his school time? Forcing obedience or saving him will get him to the following class, but what will make him become a serious student who wants to accomplish himself?

Students Have a Privileged Status

Children often hate School as they feel compelled to do work without getting anything in return. For them, to be a student appears to be slaves. This way of thinking becomes so drastic that some teens choose to drop out and get a menial job rather than be students.

By teaching your child that being a student is a privileged position, you will overcome this mindset. Let him know that others are going to be inconvenient in promoting his school success. Show him that the family can arrange schedules and subsidize any family member who needs to be serious about education. Let him know that knowledge gives the family (and society) unique meaning and significance. Finally, stress that while school success can lead to a lucrative job, learning has its quality, and it can be enjoyable to attend School itself.

The Homework Crisis

If homework problems do not occur, ADHD specialists doubt the accuracy of an ADHD diagnosis. It's no joke. Homework puts together all the triggers for most children to cause ADHD behavior.

The assignment is an incredible conflict of interest for a student. The operation requires that others provide excellent housing. When not in a class, the kid has to do schoolwork. He has to come home from a work environment and do more work instead of playing. A kid rarely feels more forced. How many kids have ever asked to do homework?

It's not shocking when your kid doesn't want to spend time to read instructions or think his assignments, or when homework is on the agenda, he sneaks, lies, and ignores. In reality, some kids feel so upset about the lesson that they choose to fail (by not doing so) rather than succumb to the perceived oppression. However, a refusal to do homework for other children is an omission of obligation or a veiled attempt to keep loved ones interested and attentive.

A Common Response

While some parents are squeamish about allowing their child to do homework because it interferes with other things, other families often have close monitoring tasks. These parents view the completion of assignments as a necessary ingredient for the success of their son. Most end up badgering their child as soon as the child enters the house to begin the task. The mission turns into a nightmare he wants to escape from. He will argue through spending hours to complete only one or two problems, and these power struggles will monopolize the entire evening. Even the smallest homework assignment can have enormous disappointment.

Increase Your Child's Control

Your child can better handle homework if he has more input about what's going on. And figure out what plan is beneficial to him instead of deciding when, where, and how he is doing his tasks.

For example, when they work, some kids do not like segregation. Allowing your child to do his job in a common area, such as the dining room, may help. Some kids prefer background music or movies. See if that works, and if it does not, revisit the problem.

Allowing your child to create their environment can also help make homework less troubling. He must find a way to do it if he decides to get it done. You know that when he intends to finish what he is doing, he is very good at tuning out distractions. Even a loud voice may fail to unglue him when he's "on a mission."

There are plenty of options for both homework and play for your son. Removing playtime before he finishes his task will make him much more resent the assignments. Unlike most many coercive activities, he'll lose focus if he feels he's being hassled, and the weakest noise could throw him off the job.

Develop a Routine

If you set up a daily routine for homework, your child will be more likely to complete his task smoothly. Like a sleep response, at a given time, his body will provide a work response. When they develop a consistent way to shoot free throws, this happens with basketball players, and your child could also get a similar benefit.

Build Independence

If your child is very young, continue doing the task together consistently during a specific quiet time. Keep him company and address any things trying to overtake him. Allowing him to remain in the lead while the assignment is completed promotes his self-management. Note you're making it more comfortable; you're not doing the work for him. For starters, you could ask his opinion on what to do first when you begin your project and check if he agrees with any recommendations you make before you continue. It reassures him that you are honoring his thoughts and finding him knowledgeable.

The more it takes care of your child, the more autonomy it gains. When he has the knack of what to do on his own, you will switch into a counter operation during homework. It takes you a step closer to completing your assignments. You might say, "How about doing my house bills as you complete some of these items in your school?" At last, you're an inch away, and without you, he completes his home studies. Let him know that his freedom will allow you to meet other tasks and give you more time to play together.

Give It a Positive Twist

Through reframing it as an opportunity to practice, you will help make your child's homework more exciting and optimistic. Inform him that just as sports practice in games and events, the assignment is like schoolwork learning. Because there is typically not enough time to learn new material or show his teacher everything he can do during School, homework can be a chance for him to improve or sharpen his skills to excel in class.

Passing in Assignments

There is yet another primary concern about the problem in the assignments. Most children living with ADHD also do not go through their tasks after completing the work the night before. Why is that happening?

First of all, if your child is used to making someone prompt him to put on his uniform, brush his teeth, and get his bag, why is it shocking that when he arrives at school, he does not pull out his homework and hand it in? When his instructor does not explicitly ask him to go through his work, it is "out of vision, out of mind."

To solve the issue, help your son determine how he will manage to send the finished task to his teacher. Help him find the environmental trigger that will enable him to turn his job around. It's a perfect time to help him work out a "success plan" that he can implement alone.

Relating to Teachers

If you have a good working relationship with his instructor, you will encourage your child's progress at school. Yet partnerships can be compromised if you consider that his instructor is incompetent or if, conversely, his teacher thinks you are not doing an excellent parenting job. That can happen if there is no contact with you. So how do you develop a relationship with the teacher of your child?

Daily Reports

Term report cards for many years have been with us. Nevertheless, it is now customary to use daily reports to track children living with ADHD. Regular updates have been widely accepted as they have some apparent advantages. Knowing what happened during your child's school day can be very helpful. Such data helps you to deal with problems efficiently and avoid them before they get worse.

Problems with Daily Reports

Daily coverage can be troublesome as educators often pull parents into issues that can be easily handled throughout the day of class. As school issues leak into the evening hours, most parents are upset. Such problems instead monopolize the family time, and parents are fearful of every report.

You can also be pushed into an official by the monitoring system. The child is likely to interpret school events in terms that put him in a favorable light, although his instructor is likely to point out that something entirely different has happened. Under these conditions, you might place a strain on your relationship with him if you criticize your son when you haven't seen what happened. On the other hand, if you are side by side with your child, you risk undermining his teacher's credibility. Sadly, if you take a stand against his instructor, you might encourage future non-cooperative activities. Your child may get the message that his teacher's conduct was inappropriate, and he may wonder if listening to her makes sense at all. In particular, if your child has often felt chastised at home, he might like the fact that you are now fighting for him instead of criticizing him. In class, he will continue to create drama because he loves your encouragement. As you can see, teacher upheaval poses the same kinds of issues as in family triangles.

Solutions

By changing the meaning of the daily reports, you will stop these kinds of issues. Instead of understanding the messages as forcing you to "inspect" and "pass judgment," see them as allowing you to "share" with your child what happened during the day. They will help you enjoy your achievements and work together to solve problems. They allow you to keep up with his life and maintain an intimate and fruitful relationship with him. You don't want to put your child on the defensive with the daily reports.

You don't want him to cover or think about the news. If you see that he did something unacceptable, ask him, "What happened when you reacted like that?" To figure out together what he needs to do to solve the problem. If it is necessary to respond to his teacher, ask him if he wants to help write the answer. When he complains about his teacher's poor behavior, remind him, "What contributed to this?" Help him understand the possible reasons for his instructor's actions and help him find a way to make the best of the situation, even though his teacher did not seem to handle things very well. Even though circumstances are complicated with his teacher, he must continue his success in class. Tell him, "How will you change your teacher?" It is helpful to say that he improves.

Chapter 22: ADHD at School

Insisting on the child's day's structure and having a routine is particularly helpful when your child starts school. Although it has nothing to do with his intelligence level, your child with ADHD is most likely to have a school problem. Although ADHD is not technically a learning disability because of their behavioral problem, these children struggle in the school system. When your child reaches the age of six and starts school, his symptoms become more apparent, and they can also begin to have more of a negative effect on his life. He will have to worry about sitting still and paying attention in a classroom setting and remembering and sometimes following complicated instructions. He will also have to deal with what is, for some children, the most difficult of all activities: interaction with other children in social situations. It also forced the child to wake up early and learn a whole new morning routine when he probably only just began to master the old one.

Work with the child's teachers and others to help your child control the disorder and get as much from the school experience as possible. Allowing your child to perform well at school is a big part of coping with ADHD in children. For your child to flourish at school, there must be a collaboration between the teachers, school administrators, and the child's parents. Teachers should be well-informed about the child's condition so everyone can be on the same page regarding his needs. Your child will most likely need a great deal of help coping with life at school because he will find it challenging to sit still for long periods as school often requires. He may get up and walk around at inappropriate times and says wrong things. He may also have difficulty following complicated directions needing everything to be explained most simply and clearly. Parents and teachers should work together to ensure that notes are taken, and homework assignments are completed.

He will also forget to record the homework assignment and to prepare for a test. Because they aren't always paying attention, they may not know about upcoming activities unless written down in his notebook by the teacher. They will be distracted by things that other students in the class are doing or even outside.

Play an active role in your child's education. Request and attend meetings at his school with his teachers and school psychologists. Make sure that you are allowed to have input and to ask questions at the conference. Find out if everyone is moving in the same direction regarding your child's education and if they are not, see what you can do to address the situation. You can also ask the child's therapist to be present at meetings to advise the teachers on the best way to get the most out of their time with the child.

Be prepared to spend many an evening doing homework with your child, who will most likely take a lot longer to complete his task than the other children in his class and who will need you to help him stay focused and get rid of distraction.

You should also learn as much as you can about your child's legal rights regarding his education. There are laws in some countries which state that your child cannot be discriminated against for education because he has a disorder. They also say that provisions should be made for that disorder in the delivery of education, in that if a special education teacher is needed, then one should be provided. The child will qualify for these special considerations once it is proved that his disorder limits his ability to function at school. In short, do as much as you can to ensure that your child receives the best education possible to reach his full potential.

Ask the teacher to keep you informed about what takes place in the classroom, whether your child is disruptive or not. Getting regular updates keeps you, the parent, informed, and able to tell if your child needs further therapy or other types of exercise.

It is also essential to let the teachers and school officials know that you have expectations for your child as far as his education is concerned. Make it clear what your goals and objectives are and work with them to achieve them. Get input from the teachers regarding how reasonable those expectations are and welcome their advice and recommendations but be alert for signs that the school has given up on your child and speak to the teachers about it right away. If both teams are not working in tandem, the child will not flourish in that atmosphere. Be careful not to compare your child to others, however. His life is not a competition. Just ensure that he lives up to his full potential.

There should be a special place established where homework is done. Make it a quiet area with no distractions, as children with ADHD are very easily distracted. The television should be off or out of hearing, and if there are other children, they should be in another room if possible. If small children in the home have the other parent or other family members, keep them organized until homework is over. Make it clear to the child that he must record his homework assignments, as they are likely to forget to do this.

While you will need to help with homework, resist the urge to do it for him, although you might assist by making the instructions more straightforward so that he can follow them. It might help divide the assignments into more manageable portions so your child does not feel overwhelmed. Take breaks if you need to so that he has an opportunity to refocus.

As a child with ADHD, you would probably have to buy extra school supplies such as pens, pencils, and erasers, because Kids with ADHD tend to forget things and are usually not very organized.

Bullying

While many parents of children with ADHD are teased about their condition at school, research shows that children with ADHD are quite likely to become bullies. There can be various reasons for this. Children with ADHD often have a lot of aggression, and they also often suffer from poor social skills. Because of their inability to fully pay attention and focus on what's going on, the child with ADHD also struggles academically. When you combine all these things, the child must feel frustrated and choose to show it by bullying other children. Because they do not feel much empathy, they would feel no guilt over taking advantage of another child to stop feeling bad about themselves and their inability to fit in. The medication would not make a difference in this scenario, as the stimulants usually given to children with ADHD do not weaken their aggression.

Parents can help decrease or stop their children's bullying habits by first letting them know in a calm and unemotional tone as possible that they have been informed about the behavior. Then they have to impress upon their child, who most likely feels no remorse, that while they continue to love him unconditionally, his behavior is unacceptable. Let him know that there will be consequences if the action continues, just as there have always been breaches of good conduct. The parent should also work with the child's teacher to find something for the child to do at school to occupy his time and give him a sense of responsibility and purpose. He could have a role with one of the sporting teams, tidying up the locker room or doing simple clerical tasks for one of the teachers or school administrators. He will feel less need to work off aggression if he is busy completing a job that he knows he has been entrusted to carry out.

Another proactive action would be to try and take him out of the situations where he is likely to bully other children, such as during the lunch break or after school. Teachers can ensure that the child spends this time in a location that is supervised. Suppose you want to go closer to the source of the problem. In that case, you can sign your child up for counseling or anger management session to teach him to control his emotions before they get to the point of violence, or if you feel you can handle it yourself, you can engage him in role-playing sessions where you teach him to respond to situations without resorting to bullying. Encourage him to talk about how he is feeling instead of acting out.

What you don't want to do when you find out that your child may be bullying is to lose your temper and scream and shout at your child. Never resort to a violent means of punishment such as spanking. That would confuse the child because how can you teach that violence is unacceptable by being violent yourself? You do not want to blame yourself either. Your child is not bullying other children because you failed as a parent. Don't react by making excuses for his behavior and finding fault with your own; that would be counterproductive. It would not do anything to alleviate the behavior and probably make it worse.

It is interesting to note that although children with ADHD tend to become bullies with more frequency than other children, they are also children most likely to have been bullied at some point. When this happens, it usually leads to an increase in their symptoms, so talk to your child if you hear or believe he is being bullied before getting to the point of frustration that causes him to be bullied himself. Talk to the teachers at his school about what is happening to take action, if needed, move him out of the situation. Be there for him, so he does not lose his self-esteem.

Self Esteem

Children with ADHD are often kept apart from the other children because they are considered disruptive. They might get into fights or be involved in bullying or different kinds of disruptive behavior. As a result, they spend a lot of time alone. Even for events such as birthday parties and other gatherings, children with ADHD might be left out because they are different at a time in their lives when children want to fit in. These exclusions and other forms of rejection can cause children with ADHD to think poorly of themselves and have low self-esteem. As a parent, it is mainly up to you to balance these negative occurrences by praising your child and rewarding them whenever they do well at school or any social situation. It could be for doing something as simple as hanging up his clothes or something more significant such as doing well on a school test. You have to work with them to achieve small goals. Give them rewards for the goals they achieve. It may not always be easy, but it's worth it for them.

What Is Self Esteem for Children with ADHD? Self-esteem refers to the individual's overall sense of liking himself or herself. It also refers to the individual's overall opinion of his or her worth and value. Self-esteem is closely related to self-confidence. Children with ADHD need to sense that they are valuable, that they have worth, and that they have the capacity to do things of value in life.

Chapter 23: Working with Schools and Teachers

During the elementary school years, most children spend more waking hours in school than with their parents. Therefore, providing an optimal school environment is an essential part of helping a child thrive, especially for children with ADHD.

Providing that optimal environment isn't easy. Many school systems are underfunded and overcrowded. You may be lucky enough to live in a great school district with adequate resources, but the recent recession has taken a toll on schools across the country. Some of the best public schools have undergone massive funding cuts or are at risk for these kinds of cuts.

Unfortunately, these cuts have the most significant impact on kids with ADHD or those with even mild attention and focus difficulties. When class size increases, there is less opportunity for individual attention. Music and art classes, where some of these kids shine the most, are eliminated. Physical education, which gives children time to use up extra energy, is also cut back or eliminated. Even lunch periods are shortened, making it harder for children to take the time to eat a healthy meal and get ready for the afternoon.

What's worse, 'No Child Left Behind' created tremendous pressure in classrooms to 'teach to the test.' Grading of schools and children based solely on test performance forces teachers to abandon creativity and individuality to produce higher standardized test scores. In this context, the ADHD or other learning-challenged child may be seen not as an individual with a unique set of strengths and challenges but as a downward pull on school test performance.

On the other hand, I am always amazed at the outstanding teachers, principals, and staff who do great things for children even under all of these pressures. I see teachers taking their time to communicate daily with parents and spend that extra few minutes with students who need help. Principals are setting up special classes or after-school homework clubs, and counselors are going the extra mile to support kids in trouble. It is the parents' task to find these resources or even help create them when possible.

Finding the Best-Fit Teacher

Judy, ten years old, was having a terrible fourth-grade year. She couldn't pay attention or finish her work; she fell behind academically and even became disruptive in class. Her parents brought her to me for a medical evaluation for ADHD.

I asked how the past years in school were. Mom told me, "It's amusing how things have gone. She had some problems in kindergarten but muddled through okay. The first grade was great, with no problems at all. Second grade was terrible—she had problems the entire year. Judy didn't want to work, got into trouble for her behavior, and fell behind academically." Mom explained that third grade was excellent; while Judy had some focusing issues, the teacher could handle her without difficulty, and Judy caught up academically. Just as her parents thought everything was settled and on track, the fourth grade had been a nightmare since day one.

What was going on? Same school, same parents, same child. Why was each year so different? It turns out that the difference was the fit between the child and the teacher.

We all know that some teachers (like some doctors, some plumbers, and some lawyers) are better than others. Even though each of Judy's teachers was competent and qualified, individual teachers work or 'fit' better with ADHD children. If your child is lucky enough to get one of them, things can go very well. If the child isn't that lucky, it may be time to intervene.

One of your most important jobs as a parent is to do your best to make sure your child has a teacher who is a good fit. To be proactive on this front, learn about every teacher's strengths and weaknesses in the upcoming grade, and try to make sure your child gets the one that is best for him. If your choice doesn't turn out to be a good fit, achieving this end may mean a middle-of-the-year switch. You may need to become a very squeaky wheel, and administrators may come to dread the sight of you. (Bake them some healthy cookies, and they'll feel better.) But don't worry about this kind of reaction because finding the right classroom for your child is worth it. Pat yourself on the back for being a good advocate for your child!

Because every child with ADHD is different, I cannot say that there is a teaching style suitable for all of them. However, I consider the following three teacher qualities to be the most important. The ideal teacher of a child with ADHD must combine a strong sense of structure, reasonable flexibility, and a positive, loving attitude. If those attributes are present, other characteristics are not as significant.

Structure

ADHD kids have difficulty staying organized, and having a teacher who is not structured will only exacerbate the situation. If the homework assignment is written down clearly in the same place on the board and homework is collected simultaneously every day, the ADHD child benefits. He or she will perform best when the classroom routines and rules are predictable, and the consequences for breaking the rules are consistent.

Flexibility

On the other hand, structure without flexibility can impede the ADHD child's chances of succeeding in school. A suitable teacher needs to be flexible enough to accommodate the child's needs and abilities, which often differ from what the teacher expects or is used to with other children. If your child's school uses one of these plans, and your child is eligible, the teacher must be flexible enough to implement and modify it based on the child's needs.

A Positive, Loving Attitude

If a child is only noticed by the teacher when doing something wrong, she will continue to behave to gain energy and attention. But if that same child receives even a short word of encouragement for the little things she does well—particularly for choices taken for granted in other children—she will do more and more things well. That is merely human nature, and ADHD children are susceptible to criticism and open to praise. That is why simply praising those things that differentiate her from other children—even when they are pushovers—may make all the difference. Anything to make a difference.

I realize that the ideal teacher may not be available, but it's your job to find the best fit possible and then work closely with that teacher to help your child succeed.

What Is the Best Type of School for Children with ADHD?

Your school choice can make all the difference for your child, particularly when that child has been diagnosed with ADHD and faces the possibility of being drugged.

Catherine was a delightful 11-year-old. She was very bright, friendly, and had a great sense of humor, but was also quite impulsive. Often she would yell out answers in class, talk out of turn, and generally disturb the teacher's equilibrium. Her academic progress was excellent, and she was talented artistically. Her parents had no problem with her behavior at home. Still, her family consulted with me about the possible need for ADHD treatment because of her classroom difficulties. My conclusion was that she was simply a bright and creative child who needed a more flexible and less restrictive school environment. Catherine's family enrolled her in a school specializing in gifted children in one way or another, and almost immediately, the problem was solved. They loved her there! Her creativity and talents were valued, and no one seemed to mind the extra talking and speaking out of turn. There was no more speculation about ADHD. The thought that she might have been given pharmaceutical treatment instead of a better placement still makes me shudder.

Here's the ideal school, in my view, for the child who does have ADHD or who is challenged with even mild attention or focusing difficulties:

The children arrive and begin the day with about 20 minutes of unstructured play. Then they go into a classroom of no more than about 20 students to begin work. Every 50 minutes, they have a 10-minute break in which they can go outside, run around the yard, or do some other non-academic, non-sitting activity. Lunch is a full 45 minutes, giving them time to eat and take a reasonable break from focused training. The school lunch is healthful and delicious. Physical education classes with organized sports and exercise happen every day. Art, music, and gardening are integral parts of the curriculum, as are science and ecology classes that involve the hands-on exploration of the natural environment.

After school, a one-hour homework club enables children to finish their homework in a quiet environment. During this time, those who have disabilities requiring specialized instruction can meet in small groups with the appropriate teachers. On most days, the children, especially the younger ones, can arrive home finished with their work to enjoy unstructured time to play and be kids.

Chapter 24: The School System and Behavior-Altering Drugs

O ver the past ten years, the number of ADHD and ADD diagnoses has increased dramatically. Now, even preschoolers are being diagnosed with this condition. It makes one question the statistics.

Why the sudden rise in ADD and ADHD diagnosis, but the methods of diagnosis remain the same? What has led to this? Are doctors making more lenient diagnoses to increase their profits, or is our youth's collective behavior changing? It may very well be a combination of both.

The primary diagnostic tool for ADHD and ADD is the observation of the behavioral symptoms. A health expert will often match the prevailing behaviors to that of a "checklist." With this kind of diagnostic tool, there is inevitably a massive level of subjectivity. It depends on the person observing if the behaviors are within ADD and ADHD criteria. The thing is, if the parent, school authorities, caregiver, and the diagnosing health practitioner put more meaning into simple behaviors, the child may easily be misdiagnosed.

In the schoolyard, children display different behaviors at different times. That is a given and also occurs in the adult world. People behave differently, depending on the time of the day, environment, energy level, personality, how they slept the night before, and a host of other factors. Some children are naturally shy, and some are naturally more outgoing. Some kids are naturally more cautious. Others are more adventurous. These behaviors are given such labels (more adventurous, shyer, etc.) because the kids are compared to each other. Therefore, a just outgoing and playful kid may be labeled as rowdy and impulsive compared to a quieter and more subdued classmate. The same child is classified as "normally playful" compared to a more active and playful child. This same behavior in the child may be accepted as standard by the caregiver, but not by the health professional. Or, the action is considered "abnormal" by the parent, but not by the school. Do you see it? It all depends on someone's perspective if a behavior fits the criteria.

Thus, can the rise in ADHD and ADD diagnosis be attributed to more attuned parents, school officials, and health care professionals? Are these people just giving more to certain behaviors than there is?

Child Growth and Development Patterns

Let us get something straight. Children are naturally playful and active. I would even go as far as to say that many kids are naturally psychotic at certain stages, which is perfectly normal. To get a better understanding, let us turn our attention to the growth and development patterns of toddlers, preschoolers, and school-aged children.

Toddlers, preschoolers, and school-aged children are at a stage when they are starting to gain independence. They are learning their capabilities by trial and error and are continually trying to test limits. They are beginning to know what their bodies can do, like running, jumping, and other gross motor movements. Slight motor movements are also being refined. Physical development is a major driving force that causes children to be more active and testy, and then you can add in the cognitive and social skills that they are starting to develop.

Children learn to interact with other people; we cannot expect them to get along with everybody instantly. It will take a few fights and episodes of shyness and arguments before they learn to deal with others harmoniously. Because a lot is going on in their brains as they make discoveries every minute, they cannot be expected to focus their attention on one particular task for more than 5 minutes (and even 5 minutes is often a stretch!). They are on the verge of discovery, and somehow, they know they have a lot of ground to cover. That explains the need to be on the move always and trying things. They have minimal experience regarding what is safe and what is not. They don't yet understand the concept of "normal" and "socially acceptable" behavior. Their little brains are still trying to wrap around the idea of limitations and safety. They learn these things through experience, and they often learn them the hard way.

Approaches to Behavioral Problems

Often fueled by stress, many people—parents, caregivers, guardians, health care providers, and school staff—forget the mentioned information. They are so focused on getting children to behave in a certain way that they forget how naturally difficult a developing child is likely to be. No rowdy behaviors, no running around, no loud voices. These adults should be caring for the children and helping them grow to their full potential, guiding them through the growing stages. Instead, they are the ones who are ruining the adventurous, exploring, and curious spirits of these children, often without even realizing it. They set rules that do not allow sufficient room for discovery, autonomy, and independence. That is especially true and becoming more and more of a problem in our public schools.

Play is a significant part of childhood development. Kids are on the road to discovery—knowing themselves and their environment. Child psychologists even use the game as a way for kids to express themselves. Young children have minimal communication skills. They have smaller vocabularies to use in expressing their thoughts and feelings. They have just begun learning the names of the things around them and still know very little about identifying feelings and managing emotions. Play is now being used against these kids. The need to play is now often seen as hyperactivity. The need to explore is now often considered impulsivity.

School authorities are now one of the "key players" in ADHD diagnosis. The staff can now give recommendations as to which child displays ADHD symptoms. It is argued that teachers can better spot the behaviors because they spend more time with the child than the parents (which is an issue within itself) and can observe the symptoms. The consensus is that ADHD symptoms tend to be noticeable when the child is with other people, such as in a classroom setting.

But with such responsibility also comes the risk of overstepping boundaries. It was evident that not all teachers and school authorities have the child's best interest at heart. Differential treatment exists in the classroom as well; it's an inevitable fact. Interestingly, more males are being diagnosed with ADHD, and a vast percentage of these diagnoses belong to families below the poverty line and amongst minorities. Many will argue that these kids receive different treatments in the classroom setting, and it has been clearly shown in studies that differential treatment heavily influences child behavior.

Some teachers tend to be more patient and understanding of one child and less so with another. The child's behavior also reflects the treatments they receive, which can turn into a vicious cycle. An ignored child will be more active and display more attention-seeking behaviors, which can frequently cause caregivers to act out of spite and treat the child differently, causing the child's attention-seeking behavior to skyrocket even further. It is an instinct. Even normal adults try to catch attention, often unintentionally and subconsciously. Hence, a kid who is ignored or receives less attention than his peers will tend to display more "ADHD symptoms" than those who receive more attention.

Classroom Controls

So a little kid who sticks his finger in a can of paint and smears it across the wall now gets behavior-altering drugs rather than being taught what behaviors are acceptable or not and given a positive outlet for his artistic instinct. An active child who loves to run around and has trouble sitting still in class is now a kid with a mental disease, who must be medicated to "control" his "hyperactive" symptoms instead of being placed into martial arts or sports as an outlet and a way to embrace his extra energy. A smart kid who is too eager to learn and blurts out answers even when not asked is now considered a kid suffering from ADHD and medicated instead of placed into a trivia program. All these kids get the magic pill and at the end of the day, what is left is a classroom of dazed, zombie-like kids with their instincts and skills being forcefully suppressed.

Who doesn't want to have a well-behaved child? A child who isn't running around, knocking things over and breaking stuff? It is tiring to care for more active kids. It is a very tempting thought to reach for a magic pill that will mask all of the energy and leave a kid who is easier to manage.

Quick fixes. That's what Ritalin and Adderall are. Instead of focusing on behavioral or nutritional therapy, schools and parents take the easy route, using drugs to artificially "control" behaviors. ADHD is a behavioral problem, which should be managed using behavioral therapy. Drugs are meant to correct a physiological imbalance (i.e., a neurotransmitter or hormonal imbalance). Even if an imbalance does exist, nutrition and exercise can often restore it, but who would want to go through all of that effort when all you have to do is ask a doctor for a pill?

Chapter 25: How to Handle School and Homework at Home

Doing Homework

Homework. All kids dread doing it. Parents encourage their teachers to give more of it because it helps monitor children and keep them busy. As parents, we have to do what we can to deal with school workload and help our children do their homework faithfully and to a high quality. That takes time and perseverance, but it is worth it. How can we, as parents, encourage our children to do their homework?

Cooperate with the School

Knowing that our child may have an ADHD problem, we must work with the School about expectations within the classroom and the School. If there need to be extensions on homework assignments, we need to communicate with teachers. They need to be aware of the situation so they can help. Asking your School to provide accommodation for your child is essential, so you should request that your School cooperate with you to support what he needs to succeed at School.

Let's look at a case study to illustrate this example:

Mr. Nicholas: Hello, my name is Mr. Nicholas. Thomas is doing very well in my class, although sometimes he has difficulty finishing his class assignments.

Mr. Park: Nice to meet you, Mr. Nicholas. Yes, I am Thomas's dad, and we need to tell you a little about his condition. Thomas has ADHD, so it is hard for him to sit still during the day. He needs frequent breaks and may require some accommodation.

Mr. Nicholas: Thanks for letting me know. What are some things I can do to help your son?

Mr. Park: You could start by giving extensions to his deadlines. He cannot concentrate for longer than fifteen minutes, so he needs more time to complete his essays and assignments. Could you give him one or two extra days, if he needs that time?

Mr. Nicholas: Sure, I would be willing to accommodate and give him extra time to do his assignments. I can give him one additional day for his duties. Which one does he need an extension on?

Mr. Park: His history paper. He has been crying at home because it is so hard for him to do. He has been taking medication; however, he is getting better.

Mr. Nicholas: Okay, I'll keep that in mind and give him more time. Maybe I could give him an alternate assignment if it is too hard.

Mr. Park: Thank you so much for understanding. I appreciate it.

In this example, Mr. Nicholas expresses a desire to understand the situation with Mr. Park's son. The son has ADHD and has been having a difficult time completing the homework assignment. And in this case, he is struggling to complete a history paper on time. The parent arranged a meeting with the teacher. They talked it over and came up with a solution to the problem. Mr. Nicholas agreed to grant his son one extra day to complete the assignment. It all started with creating meaningful communication between parent and teacher about the ADHD problem. You must provide this kind of communication to receive the type of accommodation you want for your child.

Set a Time and Place for Your Child to Do His Homework

In addition to cooperating with the School, you, as the parent, need to set out guidelines for doing homework at the house. Find a room, table, desk, or any place that is suitable for doing homework. Call it the homework room. Don't let any noise or distraction enter that room. Don't put a TV or monitor screen in that room. You can only put in a computer if it does not make any distractions and has no computer games that your child could play. Also, please find the time for your child to do his homework. Usually, that is after school or before dinner. You want to give your child some time to play immediately after class because he will likely need to burn off the energy of the day, especially after staying in a chair all day. He needs to have a break. So, schedule the time for your child's homework date.

Help Your Child Get Started and Help Them If They Don't Understand Anything

You may have to help your child get started with his homework. Many times, they may not feel motivated or have a desire to begin. But, that's where your extrinsic motivation can help them to do their work. It won't be easy, but you should get them started and help them whenever they need your help. You shouldn't just let them go off the deep end by themselves without guidance. You have to give them a structure to work within to know what they need to do. If your child has a question, be sure to answer or try to find the answer yourself.

Always be encouraging your child to do his homework. Tell him that he is working as if School is his job and needs to do good work to receive remuneration. Help your child realize the importance of responsibility and doing things the right way. Also, teach your child about how vital it is to do your homework, not only for getting a good grade but for facilitating the learning process and growing and developing as a person.

Teach Your Child How to Do His Homework Mindfully

Then, teach your child some skills that will help him to do his homework mindfully. Homework can be stressful for some kids, especially young ones, but you can bring mindful awareness to your body and mind before doing your homework or taking a test. Here are steps your child can take to do his homework mindfully.

• Sit comfortably in a chair. Find a resting position to be upright and relax.

• Place your hands down in your lap or on the table in front of you

• Sit in silence and open your ears and concentrate on the sounds coming from the room next to you.

• Put your hand(s) on your stomach. And notice how your stomach is moving up and down with each breath. Take in four to five deep breaths.

• Be mindful of how your body feels and if you feel anxious, continue deep breathing exercises.

• Now, you're able to complete all your assignments with the right amount of ease and perseverance.

• At the end of homework time, you can say to your child, "good job! You did great!" You can be friendly and kind to a child by congratulating their hard work and effort.

Follow These Guidelines to Helping Do Homework Fun

You should also make homework time fun for your child, not just work. For example, schedule a homework day in your schedule. Many times, teachers will give a lot of homework at the beginning of the week. So, on Monday or Tuesday, you could make it a homework day, where you get all your homework done on that day. Grab a slice of pizza and then have the children get to work on their task. It can help motivate them to put forward their best effort.

Monitor carefully the time that your child spends on homework. According to the US's National PTA, your child should only be spending ten minutes a night per grade level starting with 1st grade (Kristen Race, "Surviving Homework"). Suppose your child is spending too much time on homework. In that case, it might be time for you to communicate with your child's teacher about providing some accommodation in the form of extensions on assignments or less homework for your child. You don't want a task to become a burden for you or your child.

Encourage and Compliment Your Child

As your child is doing his or her homework, you must provide him with a lot of praise and encouragement. When you see that he is focusing and concentrating for longer than thirty minutes, tell him: "you're doing a great job. I see you have been working hard. Keep doing it!" Children especially need to receive a fair amount of praise to get them going and keep them doing what they want them to do. In particular, the young ones need a lot of it, because they are quite sensitive and prone to emotional challenges. And, say all of your praises and encouragement with genuineness and integrity. You must mean everything that you speak to them so that it's not like you're just buttering them up.

Take Breaks

Just as it is essential to give your child a lot of encouragement, it is also necessary for you to schedule mental and physical breaks to do the homework. Your child, who has ADHD, will likely be unable to concentrate for longer than fifteen minutes at a time. His mind will wander and be at a different place within ten minutes, so you must provide him with the time and space to go outside and get a refresher from Mother Nature. It is also essential that your child not spend too much at a desk in a stationary position. It is not suitable for your back or overall health. Don't let your child work too hard without giving him a well-deserved break. Please give him a glass of ice-cold milk or an apple to provide him with an energy boost to keep going with the work.

Establish a Rewards System to Encourage Your Child

Along with scheduling mental breaks from homework, it is essential that you also provide him with a rewards system. You should be generous in giving your child rewards for a job well done, an "A" on a test, or a diligent attitude toward studying. Tell your child:

Mom: Johnny, you did a fantastic job on your test. I saw that you got an "A" on it! Let's get an ice-cream from the 7-Eleven!

Johnny: Oh, Mommy! Thank you!

Mom: I think you deserve it because you worked so hard and studied for at least two hours for it. A job well done.

Providing good rewards is an excellent extrinsic motivation that will help your child. Getting your child to the point of a bonus can begin with a sticker chart. You can give your child stickers every day to accomplish their goal of getting the prize of pizza or ice-cream. It is often helpful for children to have a sticker chart to see their progress as they go along. Sticker charts can be used for toddlers as well as school-age children.

A good way to explain rewards to children is to make it clear to the child that doing a behavior that is required is not fun and getting a reward, like pizza or ice-cream, is fun. If behavior is required in order for your child to earn a reward, then it must be engaged in on a regular basis. Don't promise an extra special reward for extra special behavior. It does not work. It makes children expect more than they should.

Establishing what is considered positive behavior is very important. It can be a good thing to help increase a child's self-esteem. It can also be a very good thing to make a home where good behavior is natural and fun and expected. It is very important to back up rewards in a way that your child knows that you mean what you say.

Chapter 26: Taking ADHD to School – Your Child Can Be Successful Despite ADHD!

There is a stigma in the academic world against children with ADHD. Many believe that these children cannot do well in school, but that is entirely untrue. Your ADHD child can do excellent in school, and you can help them do their very best!

Stabilize Treatment

If your child takes ADHD medication, make sure they are well adjusted to one steady dose and dosing schedule before school. If they may need a change within the first few weeks of school, try to make that change a couple of weeks before school starts back after summer.

If your child does not take their medication while on break from school, make sure they restart at least a couple of weeks before the first day back. If they only take their medication during the day to get through school and wear off in the evening, make sure they can sleep if needed in the evening.

Of course, you need to be remarkably consistent with medication, which means giving it at a routine time each day. Missed doses can disrupt their ability to focus and do well in school. The same goes for therapy and behavioral treatments. Ensure you are very consistent when implementing these treatments, so your child gets the most value out of their use.

Communication Is Key

Maintain constant communication with the school. Discuss your child's problems with their teacher each year, ask them to email or call you if they have any issues or notice your child doing better. If your child has an IEP, attend every meeting with work samples that back up all points you want to make during the session. Most teachers will respect you and your child if you show them the same amount of respect.

If the school voices concerns or reports problems, address them right away. Do not put things off until you receive a bad report card or realize they are failing. Ask your child about their struggles, and get them help or adjust medication as needed. Take teacher complaints seriously since they see what your child is doing much of the day.

Stick to the Schedule

Make sure your child is going to bed and getting up in the morning at the same time. Keep their medication on a strict schedule. Ensure they are receiving meals simultaneously, doing homework simultaneously, and attending after school activities at regular times. A plan will help many ADHD children focus better, which makes them more successful.

Ensuring your child gets enough sleep and eating healthy foods is just as important as giving them their medication. Keep the communication lines open, and your child can succeed in school and their life.

Taking ADHD to Work – You Can Be Successful Despite ADHD!

Adult sufferers of ADHD have obstacles in the workplace that can put them at a disadvantage. The inability to focus on meetings can confuse and may even lead to embarrassment if they do not know what is going on and are called suddenly to contribute to the discussion. Many sufferers are incredibly disorganized, and many have trouble sticking to deadlines and turning in work on time.

All of these problems can put your job in jeopardy. They may also lower your self-confidence, which may stop you from going after pay raises, promotions, and new jobs that could bring more success to your life. An essential thing you can do to overcome this interference with your work life is to take your medication consistently or follow therapy treatment plans closely.

The Value of a List

If you feel overwhelmed with your workload and have trouble prioritizing and meeting deadlines, become a list maker. At the end of each workday, write down everything that needs doing the next day. Put these items in order or priority. When you arrive at work in the morning, start at the top of the list and work your way down. Focus only on the item at the top of the list since that will be the essential task. If something changes during the day, adjust your prioritized list, and keep going with the top item.

The listing also works for those struggling to stay focused and complete tasks on the job. Getting to check off an item on the list is a small reward that can fully keep you motivated to complete items on your list.

Baby Steps

If the organization is a problem, spend just ten or fifteen minutes cleaning up your workspace each day. Please do this at a particular time each day, so it becomes a habit. Keep a trash can in your space so you can quickly toss items you do not need. Keep a box in the area to collect things that need to be returned to someone else or taken out of the office.

Make sure you have plastic desk shelves, pen holders, and other organizational trays on hand. Everything in the office should have a place, and you should spend your pick up time putting items in those places.

Get Moving

If hyperactivity or fidgeting is a problem for you in professional settings, it may help you get up early and do vigorous exercise before work. You can burn off some energy while healthily energizing yourself for another day at work.

If you have other issues that interfere with your success at work, it may be time to see a therapist for behavior management.

Chapter 27: Reinforcements for ADHD Behavior

Behavioral Therapy at School

If your child has been diagnosed with ADHD, you need to work with teachers to help your child be the best they can be in life. Only working on your home life won't do it. It would help if you had frequent communication with your child's teacher to advocate for your child continuously.

You may want the school to accommodate your child's unique needs. The Rehabilitation Act instructs that ADHD children be allowed a quiet place to work at school and appropriate attention in class. Simultaneously, the Individuals with Disabilities Education Act (IDEA) provides that an ADHD child be given an individualized education program (IEP). The latter would be in document form and would spell out the child's performance level and the goals and services for improving it as agreed by you, the parents, and the school authorities. That will help you and your doctor to figure out the best treatment plan for your child.

This plan would be a compassionate choice you are making for your child. Their ADHD condition will be made public at the school. Can they handle that? The most challenging thing at a young age is coping with the stigma that comes from being separated from your peers. It may not be necessary unless your child is disruptive at school. You could ask the teachers to keep the changes discreet and confidential. Discuss and agree on the nature of the accommodation. It's probably better to allow the school teacher to take the lead here. The teacher knows your child better than you do within that environment, and their advice would be worth considering. The chances are that your child has been disruptive already. So if your child is isolated and made to work alone or at their own pace, it won't even come as a surprise to the other children. They don't have to know that the extraordinary measures being taken are associated with ADHD.

To help improve behavior, the teacher could offer praise when your child remains quietly seated for longer and longer periods and doesn't butt in when the teacher is talking, or another child is giving answers. The teacher should avoid situations that would affect a child's self-esteem and lead to ridicule from other children. But encourage the teacher to offer praise and rewards for work and issue a punishment for work not completed, such as detention.

Once this accommodation plan starts, ask the teachers to make evaluations and comparisons of your child's behavior and work with what went before. You will make your written evaluations of what's happening at home. Meet regularly with the school to compare notes and discuss results or anything that stands out. After all such meetings, write an evaluation report about what happened and what came up, so you can discuss it with the professionals. You can't monitor your child's progress unless you have something down in writing.

You may ask the teacher to reduce distractions by getting your child to sit in the front and away from open windows and the classroom door. The teacher should make sure your child writes down all homework assignments and shows them to you to check that they are done and sign to that effect. The teacher would also ensure that the child brings home all the relevant textbooks for assignments. You might advise the teacher to divide work assigned into little portions that are more manageable. You may also provide your child with more pencils and paper and get him to write only on one side of the paper in case he loses them. Although most children are stubborn and do not listen to you, you can make it easier on him by telling him what you want and don't want him to do.

Sometimes, some parents find that they have an argument with their child about a third party such as a teacher or a classmate. Kids can be really annoying sometimes and lack full understanding of who the culprit is. They get even more ticked off when parents blame them for a fault they did not commit. But parents should take this as a chance to show their child that he is not always right and that the teacher or the classmate is actually right. Your child will respect your opinion very much if you can show him that you understand him and accept his mistakes. This is how you instill in him that he should respect others.

Chapter 28: How to Help Your Child With Peer Problems

One thing you need to know right away is that ADHD children are full of surprises. They love surprises, but will usually not like surprises when it comes to peer relations. That is because expectations apply here AND this is the part of life where ADHD kids need to be predictable. They need to be able to trust that once they make and keep a choice, they will not discover that they actually made the wrong choice. They will need to be able to trust that what they picked will give them the constant confidence that it will be fun and not make them miserable somehow.

Some ADHD kids don't have any issue with those expectations, but most do. The reason is that ADHD kids often don't have enough experience in life to mimic social expectations applied to the other kids in the world—much less to make and keep social choices. This is the reason why so many ADHD kids with the usual external problems of being in a classroom or with trying to make friends or fulfill social expectations do so badly at peer relations.

ADHD Skills – Breathing and Relaxation

Your children with ADHD at school and adults with ADHD at work need more skills than drugs can offer to be both confident to be the most effective, alert, or successful. The enemy of productivity or performance is tension. Relaxation is one of the effective strategies for people with ADHD.

Nevertheless, this is not relaxation that is linked to laziness or extended holidays. Alternatively, this is a condition of muscle relaxation paired with sufficient excitation. Concentrated and alert, but comfortable.

Deep breathing can help relieve tension and relax. It can also help people with ADHD to better focus and remember.

Many people receiving ADHD treatment are taking stimulants. Stimulants are vasodilators that help improve the brain's performance by opening blood vessels and increasing blood flow and brain oxygen. Stimulants also help increase the development of certain brain neurotransmitters.

Deep breathing can also help add more oxygen to our bloodstreams and brains, improving the brain's performance. That is something that athletes know. Martial arts people know this. And everyone affected by ADHD must also know this.

Deep breathing on its own will not eliminate effective stimulant therapy. But deep breathing and relaxing exercises can be a critical addition to medications, and pills cannot teach you essential skills. These are the qualities necessary to achieve greater self-control.

Do this easy morning workout when you wake up and again on your way to school or work. Do this after lunch and also at school or work while coming home. And then another time to relax for the night, just before bed.

Deep breathing, as we said, can help to disable our' fight or fly' system. Those with ADHD usually are "on edge" and are often nearly at the start of the autonomous nervous system, the war or flight system.

Those who are vulnerable to excessive stress or who have ADHD-type impulsive hyperactivity need to do extensive respiratory exercises daily. Then, suppose a dangerous position in the school or at work arises, and your stress levels rise with your muscular tension. In that case, the person who has practiced those skills can start breathing deeply, turn down your autonomous nervous system, keep the adrenaline away for a while, and start relaxing.

Progressive relaxation: In addition to a calming state of deep relaxation, gradual relaxation techniques will give you the skills you need to relax and relieve stress in any situation. The right medication can help reduce depression and stress. Instead of using alcohol or drugs to relieve anxiety and stress, learning and exercising relaxing skills can achieve the same results and are much healthier.

Look up yourself as you read this right now. Take your finger and touch your forehead in the middle (from the point between your eyes and about two centimeters above). Note that place. Remember that place. Is this spot on your forehead relaxed? If not, just take a minute to relax.

You will notice that you have to relax your whole front to relax one point, and your entire face is beginning to soften. Then you start to relax your neck and shoulders. It's going to be fair; go ahead and relax.

That is a way of teaching kids with ADHD to relax. Robots to Ragdolls. It is a simple technique for progressive relaxation. Render it a match, "Robots to Ragdolls." Have the kid sleep. Then, ask the child to push his feet, "as close as they can... keep it..."

Such individuals are particularly at risk of frustration, 'behavioral illness,' poor management of emotional expression, and 'disinhibition.' That means that people with impulsive ADHD associated with just the highest muscle stress level can have emotional issues and behavior. Keep it. Hold it. Then you can relax your feet and make them as comfortable as a ragdoll.

Now calm down your feet and render them as smooth as a rag doll. "Then, get them to do likewise, with their legs under the knee, then over the knee and their stomach, tighten their stomach muscles by pushing out their stomach and then relaxing like a ragdoll. Then your back. Then the shoulders and chest, then your face."

Then ask them to lay down just like a ragdoll but take a tour of their bodies to see if there are still tense muscles. If so, tighten the muscle group and relax. Then, let the child understand with knowledge what relaxing it feels like. Combine this with a deep breath so that the child can relax further. Allow the child to stay about five minutes comfortable but alert. The more frequently the child practices this ability, the better the child can relax under stress. It is one of the skills needed to learn autonomy.

Then you have them do the same with your feet, under your knees, and over your knees. Then, for your belly, stretch your abdomen by pushing out your stomach and relaxing as a rag doll to release tension from your head, shoulders, and neck. Then ask them to lie down.

Techniques for Helping Your ADD/HD Child

Several factors must be taken into account once you know your child has ADD/HD. First, you want to understand everything you can about ADD/HD. You also want to sit down and list what it means for your child to have ADD/HD as a unique individual. Remember, this is an observational diagnosis.

If your kid has ADD/HD, your kid was born with ADD/HD. Which changed that now needs labeling? What were the stops that led to high energy, curiosity, creativity, and disability? Start a journal about your child, ask the people around your child, particularly if you don't have enough time.

Ask questions like: are there times of the day, days of the weeks, or specific situations that appear to trigger the child? Keep a food log and keep track of what your child is eating as much as possible. Are certain things triggering spikes and collapses? Or some foods that lead to action, perhaps melting? How about specific situations or individuals? Has the kid had a school year of experience in the camp where their behavior seemed unmanageable? Were there significant changes in your son's life, such as circumstances of living, gaining, or losing a close friend or family member?

Talk to your child and let him talk about their days as much as possible and compare them with what other people experienced about them that day. See where they can conclude incorrectly or grasp the larger picture of what was happening in a particular situation.

Please note that all the very bright kids have a lot on their minds and are eager to read, understand, and reconnect when bored.

When teachers or other people are pushing hard to believe that your child has ADD/HD, ask them why. To better understand what is happening, ask them to provide you with answers to the questions that you keep track of. Also, ask what they think the solutions are if your child has ADD/HD. If they want to move to a drug-based solution, make sure you know that there are advantages to drugging and managing your child more easily.

Perhaps your child has ADD/HD, so what you need to be clear about is when the gift has become an unwieldy issue and are drugs going to solve or mask the problems? Second, note that many factors may contribute to the application of an official diagnosis and a treatment prescription in your child's life. In medicine, these causes will be ignored quickly because all of the issues seem to be resolved.

When you picture your child and your child's relationship with an ADD/HD diagnosis, start shifting things and see how they help solve the problems. Start the diet, then see what changes can be made in the climate. Could smaller classrooms, more engaging methods of education, and more demanding curricula keep your child more centered and going at a quicker and more dedicated pace, both enhance the learning, growth, and development of your child and reduce labeling and prescription requirements?

When diagnosing ADD/HD in the air: dietary, environmental, emotional, mental, or even undetected physiological issues may cause or exacerbate the problems.

Is it necessary to meditate on them since we do not offer the family unit support, education, and resources? Are we medicating because the family can't or doesn't know what a bad diet is or how to support those kids? Or because the information is controlled by groups, institutions, and companies that do not have your child's best interests at heart? Should parents choose to treat their children based on the one-sided data given, or are they forced or manipulated to believe that this is the only way to act when it is not actually? Is it too easy to convince oneself (to be confident) that the fastest solution is the right one in this chaotic, speedy, insane world? In other words, that a ready meal and pill are good parents, eventually dig over the top layer if you want to know. There is plenty of information on the internet. The controlled information is what you often find first. Several research and data support ADD/HD as a diagnosis of illness on the surface and claim that treatment is an excellent alternative. Large non-profit organizations that are funded by the pharmaceutical companies that produce it. But the evidence is not so clear or conclusive when you dig deeper. Some of the studies which question medicine as a viable option are often excluded. We hear about brain scans, but only half a story. We do not hear about research that has shown disturbing questions about these boys' drugs since the data funded by pharmaceutical companies is hidden, and you must search deeper to find them.

Along the way, you can also find all the natural, one-stop shopping wonders which claim to heal ADD/HD, and you should be equally careful about them. You have to fully understand the child, build whole children's solutions, and ensure that they represent your particular child. No fast fixes, no single size fits all approaches. And if all I've said so far didn't turn your head quickly enough, I don't think AD/HD is impaired, something you need to get healed of or out of it. It is part of a process of evolution. Some children and adults are able and not disabled, learn and process differently, and are not less competent. In reality, they are often more capable of success and not a failure when setting up.

Conclusion

ADHD should be treated immediately to prevent the kid from falling behind in school and avoid causing difficulties within the household and peer groups. Without any treatment, a child with ADHD will have trouble managing his emotions, behavior, and organization skills. They find it hard to focus on one thing at a time; they need help to stay on track and to complete tasks on time. But with proper care, an ADHD child can learn to manage his skills, work on his own, and develop the capacity to focus on things that matter to him and do his work and chores.

ADHD is one of the most common behavior disorders among children, approximately twelve percent among U.S. children aged six to twelve years. It is a disorder of brain development with symptoms developing into adulthood. It is commonly found among boys, who are more frequently diagnosed with this disorder than girls. ADHD children usually have a short attention span and can't concentrate for long. They also have trouble sitting still and difficulty in organizing themselves. They act impulsively, their temper is fast, and they talk too much and act without thinking. They can't handle changes in routine, avoiding new situations and activities, and being easily excitable. With the help of parents, ADHD children can learn how to manage themselves and improve the quality of their lives.

Some of the therapy approaches are behavior treatment, social skills instruction, problem-solving training, and art therapy. Aside from medicines, parents can help their children be more self-disciplined by teaching them to set meaningful goals. Social skills training is used to improve the self-esteem of the child.

With the right techniques, children can be taught how to

succeed in their goals, become more dependable, and be more responsible. Through art therapy, children with ADHD can tap into their creative and artistic abilities and use them to their advantage. On the other hand, when ADHD children develop therapeutic skills and strategies, they are more likely to succeed in the future. When diagnosed with ADHD, a child receives a diagnosis that can affect various areas of his/her life. Each person diagnosed with ADHD is different, and parents and teachers must understand the child's strengths and weaknesses. Not every child diagnosed with ADHD is the same. Sometimes they display the same problems, but at a different severity and level. For example, some children can be diagnosed with ADHD and have inferior motor skills than their peers. These children have difficulty coordinating abilities to succeed and are unable to keep their focus. Other children have a more serious problem and are diagnosed with ADHD and have additional issues, like concentrating. These children usually have a hard time staying on task, not completing homework, or difficulty organizing their thoughts. But with the proper guidance and support, these children can learn to manage their difficulties.

Paired Associate Learning or P.A.L is one approach where the child, with his peers and parents' help, learns to organize his life and skills to his advantage. It uses planning and organization skills to teach the child how to get better at managing his work. It is a collaborative learning experience for the whole family.

Bis dolo volestotatum hillaborem vendel iunt autes ant, qui ut asitio quat quo doloruptat ad et, tem excearum dolo ea alis ent accus, ut entendae ex etur acepero erspitate rem labo. Dae si omnis perunditat es inveliq uibearcita que porpos sus ex et eos eliquate

www.ingramcontent.com/pod-product-compliance
Lightning Source LLC
Chambersburg PA
CBHW051730020426
42333CB00014B/1240